THE  MISSIONARY FAMILY

Betty Jo Kenney

William Carey Library

1705 N. Sierra Bonita Ave.
Pasadena, California 91104

Published by:
WILLIAM CAREY LIBRARY, P.O. Box 40129,
1705 N. Sierra Bonita Ave., Pasadena, California 91104

Printed in the United States of America

Cover art by Tom Fink

Library of Congress Cataloging in Publication Data

Kenney, Betty Jo, 1928—
    The missionary family,

    Bibliography: p.
    1. Missionaries—Family relationships. I. Title.
BV2063.K46   1983   266'.023   83-6572
ISBN 0-87808-193-3

89
  5   4

For Les

Contents

Foreword

This is a book written for, and by, career missionaries. It is for that committed class of persons whose call dictates that they go, learn a language, identify with the culture, live abroad for a lifetime, and carry out the Great Commission and plant the church of Jesus Christ. It is slanted for the enlightenment and preparation of those who, like the book of Job describes, must "travel to and fro throughout the earth and walk up and down in it."

Written simply enough to be easily understood, yet profound enough to engage the thought processes of the more serious, it is a redemptive book because it will help some fledgling missionary not to make mistakes that might turn him into a missionary derelict.

Mission support groups in the sending church can better understand the "when" and "why" prayer needs of the missionary family through reading this book.

I hope it will be read by many and mastered by those whose callings demand they go through with the logistics necessary to reach the lost. Jo and David, mother and son, missionary and MK, have cooperated to present this practical, warm manual for missionary living, if necessary, in some alien culture where the superficial and uninformed never go, or at least never stay. Read it prayerfully, prospective missionary in particular, with the knowledge that it bears the imprimatur of the Kenney family, who have hammered out on the anvil of daily experience every paragraph of this book. They have come through radiant with faith, confident that theirs is the greatest calling the world knows anything about, and anxious that many more share in this incomparable experience.

J. Philip Hogan, Executive Director
Division of Foreign Missions
Assemblies of God

Preface

During our home leave after fifteen years as missionaries, my husband taught classes as "Missionary-in-Residence" at Northwest College. In addition to the missions subjects in the regular curriculum, he originated five missions seminar classes, which were electives chosen by more than one hundred students. For the class "the Missionary Family", neither he nor the college bookstore manager could locate a book which could serve as a textbook. From that time Les urged me to write this book.

My first draft was a strictly "how to" manual, without reference to our family, except for the story about Irenea. Each of the three typists who worked on the first drafts suggested that I include more personal anecdotes to illustrate the principles expressed. So here we are—a family of four who have lived overseas for twenty-three years—sharing lessons we've learned, our mistakes and our victories. If our experiences, and the knowledge we've gained from scores of other missionaries, can help missionary candidates or veterans I'll be very happy.

The biggest problem in writing this book was deciding what to omit, since so much more could be said about the missionary family. One important subject, the husband/wife relationship, is treated only in relationship to other subjects. Many excellent books have been authored by Christian men and women in the past decade on the husband/wife relationship. It would be useful to have something written especially for missionaries, but I judged it too broad a subject to include here.

For college students and members of mission support groups who read this book, I have added at the end of each unit suggestions for further learning experiences. The Bibliography lists books I have read that deal wholly or in part with some of the situations discussed in the book.

I am most grateful to my husband, Lester, who took us overseas in 1958 to begin our own experience as a missionary family. He first urged me to write this book in 1973, continued to remind me how much the book was needed, and encouraged me in every way during the actual writing, trusting my judgment enough to not read it until the manuscript was finished.

Special acknowledgment however is due my son, David. I wanted to list him as co-author on the title page, but he declined, insisting, "It's your book!" I asked David to help me with the book for several reasons: to add the male viewpoint, the "single" viewpoint, the "grown-up-overseas-MK" viewpoint, the young viewpoint; and for his analytic and creative talents. David helped me to plan the outline. He then originated all of chapter 2; most of chapters 5, 12 and 14; and parts of chapters 7 and 9. He also read all that I wrote and offered editorial suggestions.

I am grateful to the scores of missionaries who have freely shared experiences and knowledge that contributed to the counsel offered in this book.

Our daughter, Joy Kenney Fitzwater, read the first draft, contributed editorial help, and suggested family anecdotes to include.

I am also grateful to Dr. Humphrey Scott, who read and approved the chapter on health. He also introduced me to the excellent reference book *Where There Is No Doctor*.

My labored long-hand pages were transformed to a neatly typed first draft; then my heavily re-written first draft became the final manuscript, under the able hands of five overseas friends; Iris Brown, Carol Kirschke, Frances Rasmussen, Sally Shaver, and Jane Barton.

PART I

In The Beginning

1. Who, Me?

"How can I know God wants me to be a missionary?" If you asked ten missionaries this question you would possibly receive ten different answers! The answers could vary from "everyone is called" to "you should receive a miraculous sign from God."

Some missionaries have received dramatic impressions that impelled them to leave their home country for ministry abroad. Others go because of a strong abiding inner sense that it is the ministry God wants for them. Some felt an urgency to become a missionary when they heard another missionary relate the ministry needs in the country he serves. For others, the Holy Spirit has quickened and personalized an appeal from God's Word such as, "whom shall I send? And who will go for us?"[1]

In our family three of us have felt called to serve as missionaries overseas. When I was sixteen, I heard our district youth leader present the need for volunteers for overseas ministry. As he challenged us, "Will you go?" I felt that God was speaking to me. In quiet prayer I answered "Yes." From that moment my long-term goal was to serve God overseas in whatever way I could. But it took 13 years to get there!

My husband responded to a challenge for missionary volunteers when he attended youth camp at the age of 18. He studied for the ministry and then served as a pastor in America. Though quite fulfilled in pastoral ministry, as doors opened to missionary service he happily volunteered. It was not a case of "I must go or I'll die!" but "I should go."

Our son David grew up on the mission field and so was exposed to missionary service all his life. From the age of 12 he felt a definite call into missions work. This call is not related to any specific event, but to a deep personal conviction that this is what God wants.

Comprehending need is basic to missionary endeavor, whether

your part is to go or help to send others. When you also have a continuing unshakeable inner feeling that you yourself should go with the gospel message, dare to respond. Continue a dialogue with God, through prayer and Bible reading, with the goal of offering yourself as a willing volunteer.

Some people fear that they are not qualified to be a missionary. Realize that you are not the first person who felt insufficient for the task set before him. God said to Gideon "The Lord is with you, mighty warrior . . . Go in the strength you have and save Israel . . ." Gideon protested, "How can I . . . My clan is the weakest . . . and I am the least in my family." God assured him, "I will be with you."[2]

The assurance that God gave Gideon is your assurance, too. If God has called you to a task, He will be with you as you perform the task. Your weakness will summon His power.[3]

You may feel unqualified to be a missionary because you have an unrealistic idea of what a missionary is. Some people believe that missionaries are super-holy or ultra-endowed. You should realize that missionaries are ordinary people like you.

During one furlough we were speaking in a church where we had relatives. I was introduced to the pre-school children's church as "a real missionary." My little cousin Phillip sat on the front row. His eyes grew big as he protested, "That's not a missionary. That's Jo!" I still wonder what he thought a missionary was, but I liked the truth he emphasized: I'm just Jo. You may be "just" Henry, or Lucy, or Pedro, but if God calls you to be a missionary, He will make you able to do what He asks.

Since this book focuses on the missionary family, the question of your family's reaction to your call is of prime importance. The majority of missionaries I have talked to felt called to be a missionary before they finished high school. While you are still in school, it is perhaps best to talk only with the Lord and your pastor about your desire to be a missionary. When you must make a choice such as college or job training that would affect your fulfilling the call, then you need to discuss your plans with your parents.

It is natural for parents to be dismayed at the thought of their children becoming missionaries. They want you to be always near them. They may have dreams of your following in their career footsteps. They want to shield you from real or imagined dangers ahead. If they have never traveled out of their country they may have unrealistic ideas about life elsewhere in the world. This is the time for you to be especially patient and understanding[4] with your parents. Do not allow yourself to argue and become angry with them. Be patient. Allow God to develop in your life the traits that will eventually help you to be a better missionary. Pray for your parents' acceptance of His will for your life. Keep your heart open toward God and allow Him to work out His will for you. In the meantime serve Him faithfully where you are.

Some people are married and have their own family before they begin to follow Christ, or before they know God wants them to be missionaries. In this case it may be that one mate feels directed to a missionary vocation before the other does. You should discuss your feelings together and be patient if your partner is reluctant to share your feelings. Give God time to speak to her (or him). In some cases the partner never feels a personal clear direction toward a missionary life, but is fully willing to serve God anywhere and happily accepts the mate's direction from God.

I have two friends who never felt a personal call to missionary ministry before they went overseas. They helped their husbands for years in Africa. When both of these women were widowed, they learned that nothing they contemplated doing was as challenging as the missionary ministry they had experienced with their husbands. Each then carried on a fulfilling missionary ministry alone. God introduced them to missionary ministry through their husband's call. Do not be afraid to trust God's leading through your husband or wife.

Recently one young wife asked me, "Did you ever have to go where Les felt you should go, without a personal direction that it was the right move for you?"

I quickly answered, "Oh, yes. I put roots down deep and they're very hard to extract!"

Though it was easy for me to go overseas originally, each move we've made to a different country in Asia has been painful. I accepted my husband's leading, though I was loath to leave the Philippines and later Malaysia. After a few months in each new place I could easily see that it was the right place for us to be at that time.

In the unhappy instance when one mate is completely opposed to becoming a missionary most mission boards advise the couple to postpone any plans for missionary ministry until they are in agreement.

In contemplating a missionary career, your children need major consideration. Though children can be a great asset to your happiness and effectiveness as a missionary, most missions will not approve volunteers with large families. This is a practical decision forced on missions by the great cost of transporting and educating children overseas.

The ages of your children is another vital consideration. Young children are usually readily adaptable to the changes brought about when their parents become missionaries. The change can be more difficult for teenagers. Those with a strong sense of adventure may be eager to go, but many young people reject any change in location. At that age their friends are extremely important to their happiness and feelings of security. If your children are strongly opposed to going you must try to understand their feelings and be patient with them. Some mission boards are reluctant to appoint missionaries with teenaged children because of possible adjustment problems for the children. If your children are already in high school and are opposed to your move, you should consider the possibility of delaying your departure until they are in college. Let God lead you. Share your feelings with all your family. Be understanding of each family member's feelings and needs. Pray together as a family until you know it is the right time for you to volunteer as a missionary.

2. *Learning to* Parlez

When you have felt the missionary call the next question is clear. What can I do to prepare myself for a missionary career? Often the first impulse is to investigate Bible schools and seminaries but this is not the only course open. There are also many things that can be done *before* going to a Bible school or seminary.

Often a person receives a missionary call while he is still young. If this happens then there are things that can be done to prepare for a missionary career while he is in high school. One of the most needed skills in missionary work is an ability to learn a foreign language. High schools and junior highs in America usually offer French and Spanish. Spanish is the language of most of Central and South America and should be considered by anyone thinking of a missionary career there. French is spoken in much of Africa, Indo-China, and the Pacific. In addition it is still considered the language of the elite throughout the world. A good knowledge of French may be the opening needed to the educated class in any country. Even if you anticipate going to some other part of the world where you would learn a completely non-European language, the skills you develop in learning any language will help you to learn another.

There are many other useful skills that you can begin to learn while still in high school. Accounting, secretarial skills, construction and mechanical skills may some day become vital helps in an area where garages are far apart and trained secretaries non-existent. Pursue any hobbies you may have, too. There is no telling what may come in handy. I know a missionary who was admitted to a country because of his ability in judo, which he had developed in a high school program. In other countries missionaries are able to minister through a proficiency in sports or music.

After high school the question of where to attend college immediately arises. Often the first choice is a Bible school but there are other alternatives that should be considered as well. One good idea is to contact your church's mission leaders to find out what school they advise and what skills they are looking for. Teachers are in demand in most Third World Countries, so there are many opportunities for a qualified teacher. One old joke says that a man who wants to be a pastor marries a pianist, while a man who wants to be a missionary marries a nurse. This is an exaggeration, of course, but there is no doubt that medical skills as well as the discipline that they require are valuable assets.

The study of language becomes even more important in college. If you go to a school that offers it you may consider studying the language of a group to which you feel called. Many large universities offer courses in such languages as Mandarin, Swahili, Malay and Hindustani. You should also consider such missions-related subjects as sociology or anthroplogy.

Most prospective missionaries choose to go to some kind of Bible college. This makes sense because as a missionary your basic task will be sharing God's Word with people. The choice of a Bible school is very important. Write to your church's missionaries and missions department to find out if there is a school that they recommend. When you are investigating the school, find out specifics about their missions program. Also find out if the school is turning out successful missionaries. A school may have a program that looks great, but because of uninspired personnel at the school few graduates become missionaries. You would definitely want to avoid a school like that.

Once you have chosen a good missionary Bible college it may be wisest to follow their missions major or minor, since it has been put together by experienced educators who know the needs of a missionary. It is a good idea to study Biblical languages in Bible college. This would be especially helpful if you would ever get involved in Bible translation work or theological training.

Many mission boards now require their prospective missionaries to attend some kind of seminary or graduate school. It is wise to check with your particular missions board to see what they require and advise. There is no use taking courses at one school which would have to be duplicated later as part of your board-required studies.

3. *I Thee Wed*

Your career choice and your marriage choice are two of the most important temporal decisions you will ever make. If you know in your heart that God wants you to be a missionary, you have settled your career choice. If you are still single, your decision on whether to marry, when to marry, and whom you will marry can vitally affect your ability to fulfill your missionary plans.

A few mission boards welcome single applicants. In ministries where an almost total time commitment is needed it can be a blessing to be single.[5] Some missions accept only candidates who are married. Some appoint either single or married candidates. Yet others will accept unmarried women, but will not appoint single men. Perhaps they desire favor from the Lord for the men! "He who finds a wife finds what is good and receives favor from the Lord."[6]

Before you meet the man or woman of your dreams . . . examine those dreams. Love and compatability bring true companionship to a marriage. This is vital when you move from home and friends. Your companion should be your "best friend" as well as the person you love most. You should be able to talk together about everything. You should know that you would be content to spend days or weeks in isolation with your partner, without a gang of friends or family coming around. A deep companionship with your mate will strengthen you for the loneliness you will face as a new "alien," or other problems that may arise when you are far from the rest of your family.

A spirit committed to following Christ is also of utmost importance. It is delightful if your companion shares your call. But if not, it is enough for her or him to be fully willing to follow God's call in your life. Before you make marriage plans you should be certain that your companion truly expects you to become a missionary and is happy to be one with you. Two unhappy missionaries wives I have counselled explained, "He told me he wanted to be a missionary, but I didn't think he really meant it!"

Be aware that you and your mate will be required to pass strict medical examinations. Good health is a must if you want to be a missionary.

A person to whom money and material gain is very important will bring upon himself much unnecessary trouble and worry as a missionary. Be sure that material possessions have a low priority in the expectations of your mate. Don't judge by what a person says, but by the things he now needs to make him happy.

Some mission boards expect both husbands and wives to be productive, full-time workers. Others do not require work of the wives, but do encourage their participation in ministry. If you marry a woman with needed skills, training and ministry gifts she can make a valuable contribution in your ministry together. But the most important qualities for successful missionary family life are life attitudes: commitment to Christ, a contented spirit, a joyful nature, kindness, trust, abiding love.[7]

4. *Pass-Fail*

Your first step in actually volunteering yourself for missionary ministry will depend on your situation at that time. If you are a pastor you should talk with the district leaders in your denomination about your desire to be a missionary. They will advise you of the next steps to take.

If you are not a pastor, but are already established in your profession, talk to your pastor. He can tell you what office to contact in your denomination. There are many openings for non-ministerial missionaries with special training (such as teachers, nurses, printers, accountants, secretaries, etc.)

If you are still a student you can write to the mission department of your denomination to learn their basic requirements. When you have fulfilled those basic requirements you will be ready to proceed with actual processing.

Basic requirements of most mission boards usually include:
endorsement of your local church leadership
a college degree or equivalent training
ordination for ministers
professional certification for non-ministers
two years experience in your profession
minimum and maximum age limits
good health
Some mission boards may also require:
graduate studies
linguistic ability
marriage
no more than three children in your family

In addition to church mission boards there are inter-denominational missions. Many of these missions minister as service agencies. Some work with special ministries (such as translators, builders, etc.). Interdenominational mission boards usually require you to be approved by your church leadership.

If you feel that you meet the minimum requirements of your chosen board and have the approval of your local church leadership, you are ready to apply to your mission board for appointment. Write a letter to introduce yourself. Describe your ministry and your experience. Inform the board of your commitment to a missionary career.

From this point you will follow steps as directed by the board. These will probably include:

a preliminary information form
endorsement from your church leadership
completing an official application
character and ministry references
a review of your college transcript
a credit report
a personal interview with you and your companion
mental and emotional health evaluations
physical health evaluation
language aptitude tests
Bible knowledge test

Should you fail to qualify at any of these points, you will be informed. It may be that you are not ready now to proceed with your missionary ministry. You many need more time and experience. Be patient. Continue in your present ministry and strive to prepare yourself more fully for ministry abroad.

The time from your first letter to the mission board until your departure for your missions ministry can easily be one to three years, even if you qualify in every respect. If there are some qualifications you must complete it can take five or more years. For this reason it is wise to not discuss your plans with your small children until you are sure of your appointment. Even one year is a very long time in the life of a small child. When your home situation is disrupted for orientation studies or deputation is a good time to explain your plans to your pre-schoolers.

It is important that your school-age children know your plan before it becomes general knowledge. Let them know that they are part of your plans.

If you have teen-agers you should share your plans with them from the beginning. They need time for the adjustments they must make. They are much less likely to be hostile to the change if they have reason to believe that you really care for their opinion about the move. Your careful consideration of the needs and limitations of your children at this point can reap years of family harmony in the future.

Our children were pre-schoolers when we went overseas the first time. Ten years later we were asked by our missions director to transfer to a different country to direct a Bible Institute. We took our children into our confidence in a family conference early in our decision-making discussions. Years later after our daughter was married she told me that our sharing confidence in them at that point made them feel a real part of our missionary ministry. Their pride in being the "first to know" made them feel important to us and greatly eased the disrupting move.

When you qualify in every respect you will probably be asked by your board to attend a missions orientation. Missions differ as to the time required. Some require a few weeks; others require several months. Some boards require a stay at survival camp also.

If your mission operates from a unified budget you may be ready to leave shortly after completing orientation. If your mission operates on the basis of pledged individual support, your next step will be deputation for raising the funds needed for your travel to the country of your appointment and your support during your stay there.

5. *To and Fro*

One aspect of missionary life that many people don't consider is travel. Any missionary family can expect to travel thousands of miles during their term of service. Not only is there extensive foreign travel, but often the family travels a great deal in America. This travel can either be a positive family experience or a problem that will bring no end of bother.

Many missionary candidates discover that before they can ever go abroad they must travel extensively in America for deputation services in churches. They may also be required to attend conferences and seminars. If the travel comes during the school year, the children should be left in school. It is too hard on a child to be taken out of school and moved around all over the country. Most families choose to leave the wife at home to take care of the children if they are too young to care for themselves. It sometimes works out for children to stay with close friends or relatives, especially if the absence is for a short time. If the trips are for the week-end only, the children may accompany their parents. It is important though, especially as the child grows older, that accompanying the parent is voluntary. Many missionary kids reach a stage in their life when they hate being identified as the "visiting missionaries' kid." They would rather stay home and attend their home church every Sunday. If this is what your child wants, be sure to respect it. Don't look upon this reluctance as your child's unwillingness to take part in an important part of your missionary service, but rather as a child's quite natural dread of being examined and discussed by a whole new crowd of people all the time. By forcing your child to accompany you, you will start out his missionary life as a negative experience. And spiritually, I suspect that your child is far better off attending one church that he likes, where he'll receive a balanced diet of the Word, than he would be jumping around from missionary service to missionary service, hearing similar presentations again and again. Of course, if the child truly wishes to accompany the parents that is perfectly acceptable, too.

If the children are pre-schoolers they can usually accompany the parents without too much trouble. Just don't forget that they don't have the stamina of an adult. Plan your trip to give them plenty of rest. It is nice to occasionally give them a rest by letting them stay in one place for awhile, either by leaving them with friends or by having the wife stay home during some of the trips.

No matter what you decide about the many trips your family has to take, traveling together in your home country can be a rewarding experience for the whole family. Our son David says, "Some of the best times I can remember as a child came on these trips." The most important thing is to not be in such a hurry to get to one place, especially if you are driving. By breaking the trip up into shorter sections you not only arrive at your destination more rested but the trip is more enjoyable. America abounds with national parks, zoos, and other things to see. I can especially remember visits to Yellowstone Park and feel that every American child is far better off for having seen some bears, deer and buffalo. As a family, pick routes that inlude things that the whole family can enjoy. It won't hurt to go a little out of your way to see an amazing site or natural wonder. The parents should also include things which will be of interest to themselves too, so that they won't get impatient with the travel. One good idea is to plan the trip ahead of time and have the children read about the places you'll visit, so that the trip will be both interesting and educational.

If you are involved in extended travel for deputation with your family you should join an automobile club. It can provide you with maps which mark points of interest. When you have time "on the road" between services you can use this time to take tours of various industries as well. Your children will have the opportunity to see America at work. They can observe first hand what many children can only read about.

During deputation our family visited a plywood mill, match factory, copper mine, cheese factory, sugar beet factory, fishing village, hydroelectric power dam, paper mill, cattle ranch, fruit orchards and irrigated farms.

Very few families have the opportunity to travel overseas as much as missionary families do. Not only will you be traveling to and fro between the United States and your field of ministry, the country where you live can be used as a base from which to travel to neighboring countries. Missionary families should do their best to take advantage of all the opportunities for travel. One of the most important things you can do is find a good travel agent to help you plan your route each time the family leaves.

Try different routes and different means of transportation to get around. Travel by ship can not only give you a peaceful journey through exotic ports of call, but can save you the bother of jet-lag, since a ship doesn't travel fast enough for this modern malady to develop. In many countries, especially in Europe, train travel is both comfortable and cheap. It is also a good way to meet the people of the country you are visiting, instead of other American tourists. Using a different route each time gives a chance for the family to see more of the world. It may cost you a few dollars extra now, but realize that many people in America save years to take a trip like this. And don't forget, *this* may be the best opportunity you'll ever have.

For the whole family to benefit from a trip, it is important to keep the whole family in mind while planning it. If you have small children, give them plenty of opportunities to rest. Have the whole family read about the places where you'll be. Reading a story about King Henry VIII makes a trip to the Tower of London far more interesting. Also, plan your accompanying luggage carefully. It is no fun to walk around carrying all kinds of bags. Carry no more luggage than absolutely necessary. Give each of the children a suitcase or shoulder bag to carry and be responsible for. Not only does it give the parents one less thing to worry about, but your trust reassures the child of his value. The responsibility helps him to mature.

Take advantage of opportunities to travel around on the mission field where you are stationed. Often these trips are the most meaningful because you know the country's background and culture. By taking their children on missionary trips parents expose them to the work the Lord is doing. There is no better way to help your child's spiritual growth than to show him the gospel changing people's lives.

One good idea is for the father to take one of his children along with him on a journey. The time together gives each of them a chance to get to know the other better. I know of one missionary who spent three weeks traveling through Europe by rail with his teenage son on the way home from Asia. Not only did they have an interesting time seeing all the places they wanted, but the time together gave them a chance to get to know and understand each other better than ever before. Of course, it is very important that none of the children is given special treatment. They should all get the chance to travel alone with their father if they wish, so that no jealousy arises.

One girl saved all her birthday and Christmas gift money in high school to be able to accompany her dad on a trip from Malaysia to Indonesia. She had to miss 2 weeks of school in her senior year to make the trip, but now, as a grown woman, she still says, "It was worth it!"

Your mission board will advise you of the legal papers you must have for overseas travel. You will require a passport to leave your country. It is wise to have separate passports for each member of the family. When you go through immigration on exit and entry, let your children handle their own passports (under your watchful eyes) from the time they are about 6 years old. If an emergency should ever require the child to travel alone he will have the confidence born of experience. Some children travel to a different country to attend boarding school. If they have been given the responsibility of handling their papers and bags while you are there to observe, it will be much easier for them when they must go alone. This is true even if they never travel alone until they return to their home country for college.

Your mission board will probably apply for a professional visa for your destination country. If your board does not get your visa, it is extremely important that you inquire at the nearest embassy or consulate to learn their visa requirement. A few countries allow you to enter as a tourist, then apply for a work permit. In many countries you will jeopardize the likelihood of receiving a professional visa if you enter first as a tourist. If both husband and wife plan to be active in ministry, inquire whether the wife needs a work permit also.

Personally check with the nearest consulate office of any country you will stop overnight in, to learn whether you will need a tourist visa. Many, but not all, countries will issue a tourist visa on arrival. Your airline usually will have accurate information on tourist visas needed. Travel agents can lead you astray in this regard. In the 23 years that we have lived in Asia we have frequently heard from other travelers that their travel agent said they did not need a visa to stop in Taiwan, but when they arrived they could not leave the airport because they did not have a visa.

You may need an official health card and certain immunizations or other health checks (such as chest x-ray). Learn from your board or the consulate what is needed. Try to have all your immunizations 2 to 4 weeks before departure, so all the family will feel well during those busy last days.

Before you leave America be sure that you have hotel reservations in all the cities where you will need to stay overnight. Your travel agent or airlines can handle the reservations. Double-check to be sure you have the reservations. In today's crowded travel conditions it can be impossible to get hotel rooms on arrival in some cities.

From your board obtain the name and address of any missionaries resident at your destination country. Write to them personally to inform them of your arrival (date, time, carrier name and number). If there are last minute changes in your departure, cable the new arrival time.

When the time arrives to leave plan to move out of your home and into temporary quarters (hotel, church guest apartment, or with relatives) one to two weeks before departure. This will give you time to take care of final details and enjoy farewell gatherings without the pressure of packing, settling utility accounts, cleaning your house, and all the other details of moving out. Realize that there will be many interruptions the last few days as friends and family call to bid you farewell.

By planning and working ahead you can reduce last minute pressures and frustrations. The whole family will enjoy the trip much more if you can avoid the total exhaustion that so often ruins a trip. Let this first big departure be a time of adventure and joy for your entire family. Your attitude can help to make it so.

More Learning Experiences

1. Interview several missionaries about their call to be a missionary. Learn at what age they first felt directed toward missionary service and what later influences propelled them toward their goal.

2. Ask active or retired missionaries what five college subjects that they studied help them the most in their missionary life and ministry. Also ask them what five subjects a prospective missionary should study today. Use these lists to draw up a list of suggested study for prospective missionaries.

3. Ask several missionary wives whether they felt a personal call to be a missionary before they were married. Ask them how they feel the wife's roles as a missionary relates to her own call. Ask how much importance they placed on a missionary call when choosing a life partner.

4. Write to the personnel department of the mission you are most interested in. Learn their initial requirements for missionary candidates.

5. Write to your church's mission board. Ask how missionaries are recruited and trained for missionary service. Ask how your church group can help a prospective missionary.

6. Invite a missionary's wife to your group meeting. In a question-and-answer session find out what special problems a wife and mother faces as she prepares to leave her home country.

7. From books on the reading list, or other books, read more on the subject in this unit that interests you most. Report to your group information that is not included in this book.

PART II
And It Came To Pass

6. *At Last!*

In all your missionary career there will be few experiences that will impress themselves so indelibly on your memory as the first departure from your homeland and your first arrival in the land of your calling. You will probably have planned and dreamed of these experiences for many years. As you approach departure your expectations for the future will buoy you up through the tedium of packing and legal clearances and the sadness of farewells to friends and family.

At this time you must be especially considerate of your family members who do not have the buoyant strength of a personal missionary call to lift their spirits as they say good-bye. Your parents will suffer to see you go, even if they fully support your going. They know they will miss you and the grandchildren. Let them know that you will miss them, and that you will write to them regularly. If your parents are in good health you can even encourage them to think of visiting you after a year or two. With today's ease of travel it is no longer necessary to always view your departure as the beginning of a 4 or 5 year separation. Many parents of modest means are now able to visit their children at least once on their mission station.

Your wife or your children may also need special understanding as you say good-bye. You can encourage your children to invite their friends to the airport or dock to see them off if it is not too far. On one of our departures our son's teacher arranged a field trip and brought his entire sixth grade class to see our ship and say good-bye. An alert and sympathetic relative who worked at our daughter's junior high school brought Joy's closest friends to the ship, too. The excitement of showing the ship to their friends eased the farewell. If your home church is near the departure place, you can let the pastor know whether it would be helpful to have members of the congregation there when you leave. We were especially blessed on our first departure when a Seattle church choir came down to see us off after their choir practice.

If you have close relatives who will not be able to see you off, be sure to make time for a quiet farewell alone with them. Assure your parents and grandparents that you will be thinking of them and praying for them when you are apart.

If this is your first trip abroad you will probably have many surprises. Most things will not be as you have imagined them. Your stops enroute to your final destination will probably be at sophisticated modern cities. If you have informed missionaries at your stop-over cities of your arrival, you may be astonished that they are not as excited about your visit as you are. In much-traveled centers such as Tokyo, Rio de Janeiro, Brussels, Hong Kong or Calcutta, the missionaries may greet new travelers almost daily. If they spend time with each one they have no time for their own ministry. If you want to sight-see in areas like this, try to arrange for tours that will not require time from the missionaries you are visiting. But do see what you can, while you can, on your own.

On arrival at your destination country you will probably be eagerly welcomed by the resident missionaries who are anticipating your help. Do not expect them all to be there when you arrive. Their work must go on every day, too.

If you come from North America where missionaries are honored, respected and "haloed" you will now learn first hand that missionaries are ordinary people who have, nevertheless, been set apart for an unusual ministry. They act and re-act just as Christians in your home church do. Perhaps, under intense and unusual pressure, they re-act more! Take them to your heart. Listen to them and learn. Do not counter their experienced advice with your knowledge gained from much reading!

Your reception by the country's nationals can vary immensely. If you go directly to a language learning center your arrival will cause little reaction. The believers in the churches have seen many new missionaries come and go. It is no special excitement to have another one arrive. Other residents in the city will be accustomed to seeing many foreigners of which you are just one more. So what?!

If you go to an established ministry where your skills have been long awaited, your arrival may be more eagerly welcomed. Perhaps a welcome service or dinner will be held in your honor. Beginning now and continuing "forever" it is important for you to eliminate certain phrases from your vocabulary. Never refer to your host country as "the mission field." Never advise "In America (or Canada, or Korea, etc.) we do it this way." Do not make ethnic jokes, even about yourself.

Avoid "airport expert" analyses of the people or place. Make no political references at all. Also, make no references to other religions. You can extol Christ freely without speaking against other religions.

If you go to an area where there is no established church you may be received with indifference or even hostility. In this situation your home and family will be your haven. But as you "love your neighbor as yourself" you can break down hostile or indifferent barriers and find an entry for the gospel. When we settled at our first mission location the neighbors were hostile. Our house was actually stoned night after night! But when we left four years later all of the neighbors were congenial, several were close friends. We'd been able to minister to them in times of distress and share Christ with them. And all of the children (26!) attended our vacation Bible school the last year we were there. We were well aware that it was the friendship that developed between our children and theirs that changed their hostility to acceptance. Your children can be effective ambassadors of good will as you settle in your new home.

7. *White Ghosts*

When we had been missionaries only a few months another "new" missionary family visited us. The wife asked me, "What is the most difficult thing about missionary life for you?"

Without hesitation I answered, "Being an alien."

To look, and sound, and feel so blatantly different from everyone else is quite a shock at first. The more homogeneous the people of your new home area are, the more different you will appear.

While he was in the South Pacific, David went with friends to visit their relatives on another island. Although the island had been visited many times by westerners, at that time he was the only Caucasian on the island.

After dark one night, as they sat together talking, the village generator broke down. The entire village was plunged into darkness. His friends soon began to laugh because his white skin made him the only person who could be seen in the dark room. One of them went to the door and called (in their language) to the children who were playing outside, "Come see the White Ghost sitting in here!"

They all laughed together and from that moment on he was "the White Ghost" to his friends in that village. This humorous incident is a reminder that, wherever you go, you will be "the white ghost", the different one. It is *your* responsibility to observe, understand and adapt to the culture of the people you live among.

Many books are available that can help you to adjust to a new culture. (See Bibiliography) You should certainly read the books your mission recommends to you. In this chapter we will discuss only a few areas of adjustment and how your reactions can affect your family.

From the first day of your arrival it is important that you maintain a positive attitude in your home about the differences you will encounter. Your children will quickly pick up attitudes or criticism, suspicion, or disapproval that you show or express. When you are tempted to criticize an action as "rude or thoughtless", remember that the action may be considered rude only in your own native culture. It may be perfectly acceptable to the people of your new country.

For example, many westerners consider a "place in line" an inalienable right. Let the person beware who tries to "jump the queue"! Yet in some cultures your status in society determines whether you need to wait in line or move to the front immediately.

When you see an action that disturbs you, observe whether it is common behavior. Try to understand why your attitude toward the action is different. Three areas where you may encounter differences are body language, physical contact, and giving and receiving gifts.

One new missionary told me, "I never thought I was jealous, but when I see these men staring at my wife, I feel jealous and angry!" In his background, staring was considered rude or suggestive. When he learned that staring merely expressed friendly curiosity in his new culture, he was no longer distressed by the stares of strangers.

Remember that your body language can also cause distress to the people you now live among. Some actions that are common among westerners (such as combing their hair in public, crossing the legs or ankles) are strict taboos in many societies. Especially when you sit in front of people in a church service be careful to sit and stand in the same way the national church leaders do.

Many western speakers point their finger at the congregation as they emphasize something in their message. In some countries this is a great insult. In much of Asia you should point only with the whole hand extended.

When you sit in a group observe how the local people place their feet. If they are tucked back under the body it will be wise for you to tuck your feet back also. To sit with your toes pointed at someone can be an expression of disdain, condescension, or worse!

How can you avoid making a terrible gaffe as a newcomer? Perhaps you can't! But it will help if you:

Remember: *You* are the strange one.

Observe: What body movement is common to you that you never see a local person doing?

Inquire: As soon as you have a local friend, ask him to tell you if he sees you doing something that is strange and unacceptable in his society. Receive his advice graciously without defending your action and he will continue to help you.

If your manner is gracious the people will usually forgive your *faux pas* at first, but they will expect you to learn.

It has often been said, "Everyone understands a smile!" True, but people in different cultures understand different meanings from a smile. To you a smile may express friendliness, amusement, approval or pleasure. In another society a smile may express only ridicule. And in yet another large part of the world a smile means that you are proud of your beautiful teeth and want everyone to see them! The person who doesn't return your smile may not be unfriendly at all. Perhaps he is very kindly refraining from showing you that actually his teeth are nicer than yours!

There are great differences between western attitudes about physical contact and those of other lands. One Southern Asian told me, "the most difficult thing for me to adjust to in the Christian church was 'shaking hands'. In my culture a man never touches any woman except his wife. He never touches another man except to hit him in anger."

In some cultures the head is considered inviolate and should never be touched by anyone. A South Pacific islander told me some of the first missionaries to his area were killed because they patted children on the head—a great taboo. In Thailand today you should not touch a person's head.

In some western churches people are encouraged to express love by a handshake, an embrace, or even a kiss. In many cultures to do this would be extremely offensive. Remember, you are the different one! Accept the "touching" mores of your new culture. Do not try to teach them your ways!

On the other hand, the people of your new culture may touch in ways that are new to you. In many places men and women (even husbands and wives) never touch in public. If you hold hands with your wife or kiss her publicly you can cause great embarrassment to the people who see you. However, in some countries, men with men, or women with women, quite commonly walk along holding hands. This has none of the bad connotation that it might have in the west. It is only an expression of camaraderie. Be careful to avoid making judgments based on your different culture.

People of different lands express interest or affection for children in various ways. In one country we've lived in adults expressed admiration for a child by gently pinching his cheeks. Small babies will readily accept this, but toddlers and older children may recoil from a new kind of touch. I have heard parents even complain about it in the presence of their children. Then, naturally their children show hostility when touched. If the parent explains that this is the person's way of saying, "I like you," the child will learn to be gracious. If you help your children to learn the new ways quickly, they will help you into the hearts of the people. Observe how the people of your new culture show affection or approval. Tailor your own expressions to others so they will be correctly understood by everyone. In many cultures much praise or show of affection is considered excessive or phony. Learn to fit in and help your family to adjust.

In some cultures one hand is considered unclean. This is often true among people who eat most of their food with the fingers (without spoons, chopsticks, etc.). The left hand may be used for all "unclean" tasks. The right hand is used for eating. Thus, it is a great insult to offer or receive an object with the "unclean" hand.

Remember! Observe! Inquire!

Among people who regard one hand as "unclean", a gift must always be offered and received with the "clean" hand. Others always offer or receive a gift with both hands. Observe what other people do and do likewise.

Americans usually open a gift in the presence of the giver and thank the giver profusely, "ohing" and "ahing" in great admiration of the gift. Conversely, the giver of the gift usually downgrades it: "here's a little something", "just a small token", "it's not much, but . . ." In another culture the giver may emphasize that it's the best he could give you (for you are very worthy). The receiver in turn shows little response (since he is unworthy to receive it). In many countries, to open a gift in the presence of the giver is considered very rude. It seems to the people that you are more interested in the gift than you are in the one who gave it to you. Also, among some people you will never be thanked for a gift. The receiver may tell others how good you were to give him the gift, but he will not tell you. After all, "It is more blessed to give than receive", so you have already been blessed when you gave the gift. Remember: do not judge another's gratefulness by your cultural patterns.

In some cultures you should never visit a home without bringing a gift. In others you would offend by bringing a gift. Inquire!

Americans are occasionally thrilled when an Asian gives them as a gift something they have greatly admired, such as a scarf or small piece of jewelry or house decoration. The westerner did not know that his profuse admiration put his host under obligation to offer the item as a gift. It was then the guest's obligation to refuse the gift, but he did not know this. It is extremely important that you quickly inquire and learn the "rules" of gift asking, giving and receiving. Help every member in your family to adjust to these rules in order to avoid offense.

An American friend visited David at one of the countries where he was teaching in the South Pacific. He repeatedly mentioned to David's friends his admiration for certain items of local handicraft. He told them that he wanted to buy some before he left. As soon as David and his American friend were alone, David explained how the comments place his local friends under a social obligation to buy those things for him. Also that his continual commenting on the item's desirability would appear to them as rude and obvious hinting. Of course that was not at all intended! His friend wisely appreciated the counsel and defused the problem by avoiding further discussion of the items he admired while David's other friends were around.

Keep an open attitude toward new customs. Be willing to learn the reasons behind the custom, or if the reason is long forgotten, at least to accept the custom as a way of life in your new land. If your attitude is positive your family will find it much easier to adjust happily to their new life. If, in the home, your attitude is negative and you often express criticism, disdain or condescension toward your host culture, you may sow seeds of bitterness in the hearts of your children.

As you learn the ways of your new land you may find customs that are directly opposed to your native culture. In this case, you should help your children to understand the reasons for the difference. These "culture clashes" usually result from two people looking at similar situations from completely different perspectives. Help your family to realize that neither way is necessarily "right" or "wrong", "superior" or "inferior". It is two different customs, each correct in its own place. If you over-emphasize the correctness of the new way, you may intensify re-entry adjustment difficulties for your child when he returns to his native land. With a positive attitude toward both the new culture and his native culture you can help your child adjust now and also help him through the identity crisis he will face in the future on return to his native land.

8. This Is A Castle?

Your first home in a new country may be a temporary home for the time that you will be studying language. You may even find that it is necesssary to move several times in your first term. It is important for family stability that you learn to quickly make a new location feel like home. Even if you are going to stay in a place just a few months, try to give it the personal touches that will identify it as your home.

Myra Scovel, missionary to China and India, recounting their many moves,[1] told how they always packed treasured living room decor last and unpacked it first, so their own imprint was immediately established in each new home. Their treasures included a snow scene landscape that had hung in their grandmother's home, antique wrought-iron candlesticks, and the family clock, affectionately called "Aunt Martha."

A clock was one of our "movable roots", too. A gift from Les' mother, our little Black Forest cuckoo clock had scheduled events for our children from their earliest memories. "Let's have our story and prayer time now, so when the cuckoo calls seven times you can hop into bed!" "When you count twelve cukoos it will be lunch time." When they were older: "We'll start school when the cuckoo says it's 8 o'clock." When we moved to Hong Kong our cuckoo caught laryngitis from the salt-laden breeze that blew in from Tolo Harbor everyday. After the clock was repaired (and the repairman warned that it would be the last possible repair) the poor cuckoo had a croupy rasp on the sixth "cuckoo", but stayed on the job for a few more years. When it finally died, after marking 26 years in four countries for our family, we let the dear old bird hang "in state" for 2 years before we could bear to "put it away."

Another frequent mover, Shirley Moore,[2] said they offset the fear that their family would lack the security of old home traditions by carrying their traditions around with them. Battered but beloved stuffed animals, much read books, and "oodles" of albums of pictures made up the "attic" they carried with them.

Look around your house. Does your family have some small items that spell "home" for you? Take them overseas with you. Even grown-ups get comfort from such a security blanket! It is a good idea to take with you pictures of your children's grandparents which you can set up immediately upon establishing a home. It may be comforting to the family at first to have pictures of the home they left behind, also.

In mission locations you can find a wide variety of living

conditions. If you go to a large modern city you may live in a home just as nice as any home you have ever lived in. If you go to jungle camp for survivor training, you may find your first home very simple. It is important for you to realize from the beginning that you can make the home "your castle" and give your family a feeling of warmth and togetherness regardless of the material value of the surroundings.

The style of home you choose will depend on where you live and the financial standing of the community you will serve as a missionary. It is not suitable to live in a home that is far above the value of the homes of most of the people that you serve, nor is it suitable to live more poorly than is required for your standing in the community.

I once inquired of my language instructor, "What do you think is a suitable home for a missionary?"

She was not a member of our church and felt very free to comment on missionary life-style. She answered quickly, "It is not so important whether the home is very fine or very simple. The important thing is whether we feel welcome in your home."

If you can establish in your home a warmth of welcome and hospitality, an open heart, your home will be a blessing to you and to the people you serve.

If this is your first visit to another country you may find the furnishings very different from those to which you've grown accustomed. I remember how I laughed inwardly at the funny little kitchen stoves, with the broiler perched high above the stove top, when we bought our appliances in Malaysia. Years later I was still laughing: with joy over the ease of broiling without standing on my head; with satisfaction over the economy of a small oven and burners that used half as much propane gas as my friend's American stove did.

It can be helpful if you do not need to establish your permanent home immediately. If you are in language study or in an area for a short term you may live in a guest house. Or you may live in what is usually called a "leave house." this is the home of other expatriates who rent their house out while they are on home-leave. This gives you an opportunity to become familiar with the type of furnishings that are most practical in your new country. For example, you may like overstuffed furniture because that's what you used where you lived before. But in your new country it may be very impractical and hot. You would soon tire of it. Give yourself a little time to live in your new land before making major purchases other than the things you need immediately, such as a refrigerator. When you do buy, choose furnishings that are practical, convenient and attractive. You may even need to make (or have made) all your furnishings!

Your home will reflect your personality. A family in which all members are very gregarious will be open to all and may even sometimes seem like Grand Central Station. Other families feel a greater need for privacy. Their home may become to them somewhat of a retreat. Perhaps a good compromise is to have part of your home that will be open, where everyone will feel welcome to come and visit, and keep part of it private for your family. This is especially important for people who are in institutional work, where great demands can be made on their time by students or others whom they serve. You may need a private corner where you can be alone with your family for a time of play, or work, or quiet. If you need this, don't hesitate to make a corner of your home a castle retreat, safe against intrusion or invasion.

If your home is located in the tropics, several unseen families may have claimed it as their home before you arrive! Although the house appears to be very clean, before you move in anything, have it thoroughly fumigated. You may be able to hire "Pest Controllers." If not, buy a strong disinfectant from a provision or hardware store or gas (petrol) station. Wear a wet cloth as a mask and thoroughly spray floors, closets, drawers, cupboards, and foundations. You'll be amazed at the families you'll dislodge: centipedes, silverfish, cockroaches, ants, scorpions, lizards, mice, etc. If you are in a termite-infested area, make monthly inspections for termites all around the house foundations. These wily invaders can find their way through the seams of file drawers and march right through your permanent records. I've seen it done! It can be a battle to defend your castle against pests, but it's not impossible. Ants and lizards may even fight on your side! Ants carry away the dead, and lizards catch moths and mosquitos.

If you have moved from a temperate zone to the tropics you will encounter constant high levels of heat for the first time. High humidity coupled with heat create some problems around the house that may be new to you. These ideas I've learned through the years may help you to cope with heat and humidity in your home:

Nursery: A common problem is prickly heat, especially with babies and toddlers. If you can sleep in air-conditioning it will almost eliminate prickly heat. If you can't, try using Dial soap and medicated baby powder. Someone told us about Dial soap on our first trip out and it worked! If you can't buy it, contact your church support group. They will be happy to send you some.

Bathroom: An annoying result of high humidity is the souring of wet wash cloths and towels. Rub some soap in the wash cloth after you use it, to deter souring. Unlearn your neat "fold and hang" lessons. Hang towels and cloths fully spread. Put a wire across windows to hang wet cloths on if you can.

Kitchen: Keep bread in the freezer to prevent molding; the refrigerator hardens bread. Store wrapped cheese in the vegetable crisper for correct humidity.

Living Room: To keep dampness from wall hangings, incline pictures a little from the top and use little wedges at the lower corners to push the frame out from the wall a bit.

Laundry: Wash damp items immediately or dry them before you drop them in the clothes hamper. To remove perspiration stains rub detergent into stain. Wash in hot water with chlorine bleach. If fabric is discolored, treat fresh stains with ammonia or old stains with vinegar, then rinse and launder.

Dining Room: If you have a few treasured pieces of silver you want to have on "on view", put them behind glass, with some camphor in a dish near by. The camphor greatly retards tarnish.

In fitting in with the situation in the country where you locate, you may also find that it is considered proper for you to have domestic help. This may be the first experience you have ever had with someone working in your home or permanently in your home. Since this presents a very large change in way of life for most Western missionaries, we will further discuss domestic help in the home in a later chapter.

It is crucial as you set up your home that you remember the limitations of your budget. Your mission will probably either have a mission home which you are required to live in or will furnish a maximum rent allowance for you to rent a place. From the beginning, carefully figure whether you are fitting into the budget you have for a home.

There can be hidden expenses that you are not aware of from your previous renting experiences: utility deposits and payments, key money, servants' quarters, maintenance fees, property taxes (passed on to you as "rates"), guard. Meticulously inquire of the landlord, and get in writing, all expenses for which you will be responsible.

In the more than 20 years we have been missionaries I have seen certain mission houses change occupants several times. It interests me every time I visit a "new family" in one of these "old homes" to see how the family has put the imprint of their personality on the home. The type of home is not so important. The value of the furnishings is not so important. The important thing is how you make it "your" home. Your use of color, your choice of decor, the way you arrange

things will identify it as yours. Try to establish the homey feeling as
soon as possible. Then when you must move, leave up those things
that make it your home as long as possible, in order to keep the
feeling of a settled home.

9. *Solo*

I regularly attend a prayer conference with other missionaries in
the Hong Kong Evangelical Fellowship. Of 192 missionaries there
are 71 married couples, 49 single women and 1 single man. The
one single man is a widower. Many of the single women are teachers,
nurses, or doctors. Most of them have never married.

In our own mission, world-wide, of 1230 appointed missionaries,
134 are single. This number includes five widows and one man. The
rest are women who have not yet married.

These statistics illustrate the fact that singles, particularly women,
contribute strongly to mission ministry. Some single missionaries
enjoy the freedom of living alone. If you are in a high pressure
ministry or a heavily people-oriented work you may need that quiet
solitude at home. If you expect to live alone, take with you things that
will enrich your hours alone: a few really good books that will bear
much re-reading, art or craft supplies, table games, puzzles, a cassette
player and good music cassettes. Even if your work schedule is very
tight, if you live in an underdeveloped country you may have
household help that will free you of household chores and give you a
few leisure hours.

Economic factors force may singles to share quarters. Or they may
prefer companionship in the home to solitude. If you want to share
quarters with others it is wise to get acquainted before you decide to
"move in", if this is possible. Some personalities do not mix well on
an around-the-clock basis!

When you share quarters it is important that financial
arrangements be agreed upon from the beginning and mutually
adjusted from time to time. The same applies to work responsibilities
in the home.

Establish an open relationship so you can freely discuss any
differences that arise. Living with others requires "give and take" by
everyone. Make an early attempt to solve problems. Festering
dissatisfaction can wreak havoc with your home life. Try to avoid too
much dependence on each other.

Whether you are single or married, the relationships that you
establish with other misisonaries are vital to your adjustment and

happiness while you live overseas. Other missionaries working near you may be older couples whose children are gone from home, young families with small children, or singles. Unless you make a conscious effort, you may find yourself mixing socially only with those who are of your age group or your type family, neglecting the friendship of other missionaries.

If you have come from a large church in your home country there are usually ministries designed to meet the social needs of families and singles separately. But in your new mission community, you may need to pay particular attention to the needs of the young family, the older missionary, or the single missionary. A secret to appreciation and happy working relationships is that each consider the needs of the other rather than his own.

The single missionary can be a real blessing to families whether they are near the same age or different ages. In many mission stations it is common for the children to speak of missionaries as "Aunt" and "Uncle." In many cases a true aunt or uncle relationship develops. Older missionaries can fit in as "grandma" or "grandpa" with the children of young missionaries. Single missionaries can supply the needed role of aunt and uncle, while the young family provides companionship for the single, too. Marilyn McGinnis[3] advises singles to spend time with families as well as other singles, with the sage caution to "keep your distance" from a couple whose own relationship is strained.

Older missionaries can be a great encouragement to younger ones, both married and singles. In our first term, as a young family, the older couples in our area were warm and welcoming. Their genuine friendship quickly dispelled the "ogre" stories we'd heard at School-of-Missions about fierce "senior missionaries" who eat new missionaries! Our pre-school children loved them as dearly as grandparents and eagerly anticipated their every visit.

Families need to be aware of the social needs of singles. It is easy to get so involved with your own family activities that you fail to share your blessings with someone who is lonely and needs your friendship.

In the case of single missionaries there are two social problems that can develop. These problems especially occur when the single missionary is stationed far away from other missionaries, or there is a big age difference between the single missionary and the missionary couples. The first of these problems arises as the single missionary begins to find close friendships with the people of the host country. As a result of these relationships the single missionary may develop a much greater sense of identity with the customs and society than the married missionary, whose closest relationships are still with members of his own culture (that is, his family and missionary friends).

This development can be immensely helpful to the mission as the single missionary can often help to bridge the gap between missionary and national. Unfortunately, the opposite often occurs. The single may develop resentment against the other missionaries and begin to feel that he is the only missionary who truly understands the local scene. The single missionary must be on guard against such feelings. It is helpful to realize that you are also an outsider and that your viewpoint is not necessarily more valid than any others. In fact, the single's viewpoint is often a reflection of the view of his close national friends, who may not be expressing the view of the majority of nationals. Married missionaries can help to avoid this problem by being open and friendly enough with the single missionary to keep this adversary relationship from developing.

The next potential problem develops as an extension of the first situation. This problem comes up when the single missionary beings to develop a romantic emotional relationship with a national of the opposite sex. Each mission which has single missionaries should realize that such relationships are virtually inevitable. Clear policies should be set and made known to singles before they go overseas.

It is important that each person is aware of the way he can serve the other and is careful not to take advantage of the other. We are naturally self-centered creatures. It is necessary for us to be alert to the danger of wanting our own needs fulfilled, but ignoring the needs of others. For example, the missionary with the young family may expect the single missionary to babysit for them while they travel or go out, without doing anything in return for the single missionary. Or the single missionary may expect to be included in holiday meals or regular family meals as a matter of course, without expecting to do anything in return for the family.

If you feel that you are being taken advantage of, it is a good idea to list all of the things that you do for the other missionaries in your area. Then list also all the things that each missionary does for you. You may even have a conversation with the missionary in which you talk about the ways that you bless each other. It is so easy to take for granted what others do for us, but to feel greatly imposed upon when we must do for others.

It is quite natural that in a community there will be some people whom you will enjoy being with more than others. It is very good when you can find congenial people with whom you can spend time. Friendship is a treasure wherever you find it. Just be careful not to ostracize those particular members of the community to whom you may not be attracted.

You may sometimes feel slighted because some of the missionaries on the field spend most of their time with each other and never socialize with you. In this case, make sure that the fault is not yours. In one case, a missionary couple felt frustrated because they felt they were being left out. Missionaries who lived in another part of the country often visited the missionaries who lived near them. Finally, in frustration, they asked what they had done to offend the visiting missionaries. They felt that surely there was some reason why the visitors had never "dropped in" on them. The answer was simple. The couple hadn't ever invited the visitors to their home, so they were hesitant to impose. Before worrying about why others are avoiding you, ask yourself if you are being hospitable to them.

Singles should plan their vacations carefully. If they enjoy being alone they may like to travel alone. If they feel lonely, discouraged and homesick when they are alone, they should plan their vacation and social times to be with people. Singles should not expect to always be the guest. They should feel free to entertain other singles, couples or families in their home. One single missionary told me that she always makes it a point to invite two couples to her home for dinner so that the two men will have each other to talk to and she will have the enjoyment of conversation with mixed couples. She is determined not to drift into a life-style where her only social contacts are other women.

Perhaps as a hang-over from an age when men weren't expected to know how to cook, men who are alone are invited to join family gatherings or couples more frequently than single women are. If you want to be included in social functions and find yourself left out, initiate your own plans to which you invite others.

Holidays that are typically "family" days can be a hard time for the single missionary. One woman told me that after waiting with bated breath every year—"Will anyone invite me for Christmas this year?"—for four years (and being invited each time!) she decided to have Christmas in her own home. She invited two other singles and a couple. The couple came from a distance and stayed 4 days. It was wonderful! She could have everything like she wanted it, like home! She wondered why she hadn't thought of having Christmas at home before.

One missionary told me that the greatest loneliness of being single is the feeling that no one shares your ministry vision. He learned by experience, though, that when he expressed interest in another person's ministry, the other person often reciprocated by sharing his vision.

One single missionary told me that when a single missionary lives with a family, relationships are greatly enhanced by: clear verbal and nonverbal communication, understanding each other's needs, mutual respect. How true, for families as well as singles!

Have you decided, either through necessity or personal choice, to make your missionary journey a solo flight? It will be rewarding as you continue to commit your way to the Lord. To help you in working out a happy and fulfilling career, a single woman missionary has written a book I highly recommend, *Single and Satisfied*.[4]

10. *Dear Mom and Dad*

In the excitement of arriving at your new destination it may be easy for you to neglect your distant family for long periods of time. It is very important that you maintain a close relationship with your family that you left behind. If your parents are there, they may be greatly worried about you. You have traveled to a country that is unknown to them. They may have vivid imaginations of privations that you are suffering. As soon as you are located in your new country, take pictures of your home to send back to your family. Let them know the nice things about the place where you live. Send them pictures of your way of life so that they can understand that things are well with you.

When we went overseas it was very hard for Les' mother. She was a widow and he her only child. One day shortly before we left I overheard her say to herself sadly, as she watched our children play, "Poor little children . . . no one but savages to play with." Then I realized the worries she was suffering.

When we arrived at our first posting, a city of 140,000, we wrote to tell her how nice it was, but still Mother worried.

In our first service a lovely young lady came to the altar to accept Christ. We learned that she was an accomplished pianist and piano teacher. She became the church pianist and taught our daughter Joy. After a few months her students had a piano recital. It was an elaborate affair attended by more than six hundred guests. The students all dressed beautifully and a professional photographer took pictures of the group and each performer with the teacher. When we sent grandma a picture of Joy with her lovely poised teacher it allayed all her fears of the "savages!"

Of course you may not live in a nice city; you may live among tribal people. But you can encourage worrying parents by telling them the positive things about your new life.

Try to write to your parents at least once a week. Even a very short letter is news that you're all right. Remember your distant family! It is harder on those who are staying at home, than you who are traveling, because you have the excitement of new experiences.

If you are an older missionary and your children must be left in your home country, or travel to another country for studies, carefully nurture the ties with your children as well.

I remember vividly a friend whom I knew in college. At the end of our freshman year she wrote in my yearbook "Thank you for your friendliness to a sometimes lonely girl."

When I returned to school I made a point of spending more time with her. She told me that sometimes she didn't hear from her parents (who were missionaries) for as long as three months. They were just too busy to write! She missed them and was often very lonely.

It is extremely important that you nurture your ties with the distant family. Write regularly to your parents, your children and other members of your family. If you and your distant family agree that once a week is too often, do establish a regular interval when you will write. Keep those ties strong and you will find great comfort from these relationships through the years that you are away. More important, you will be giving comfort to those members of your distant family who need their contact with you very much.

11. Return to Paradise

A standard joke that circulates among missionaries is the young person who is "called to be a returned missionary"! Certainly the elation of returning "home", after several years away, is as great as the excitement of going out the first time.

However, as departure time nears, you will find that your roots have gone much deeper than you had realized. It will not be easy to leave people you have ministered with for several years. You must leave a large part of your heart behind!

The move can be traumatic for your children. If they were small when you arrived, they are now leaving the only home and friends they know. They don't have the "home" memories you have to help tug out their roots.

David was just 6 years old when we returned after our first 4 years overseas. When we were at the airport he was sitting very quietly while we chatted happily with all the church people and other friends who were there to see us off. The other Americans there asked David, "Are you excited about going back to America?"

I was startled by his sudden, sure, explosive, "No!"

We then boarded the plane and as it took off David burst into tears. As soon as we could remove our seat belts I went to sit with him. To my wondering "Why?" he sobbed, "We're leaving the best people in the world!"

He couldn't be comforted. This little boy who almost never cried, even when spanked, cried great tearing sobs that broke my heart. How poorly I had prepared him for this uprooting. It took much reassuring that we would come back "when you are 7" to calm him.

When we had our required physical examinations that summer the doctor told me that David had a functional heart murmur. He assured me that is was not serious and would probably correct itself, but he was curious whether David had gone through some traumatic emotional experience that might have caused it!

Start early to prepare your children for their departure. Ask relatives and friends at home to send you pictures of the children their age who will be their new playmates. If possible, get pictures of the school and church they will attend on furlough. If you plan to return to the same area, talk about this to reassure your children.

Try to avoid speaking of your homeland as if you were returning to "heaven." Usually the longer a person is away on his first trip abroad, the more he idealizes what he left behind. If he leads the children to think that they're returning to a land of paradise, they will be in for a rude awakening on arrival.

One missionary told me that their children missed milk dreadfully when they were in the tropics. She assured them that when they got to America they could drink all the milk they wanted. On their arrival with four growing boys she found that they simply couldn't afford to buy all the milk the children wanted! They were hard pressed to keep their promise. Try to avoid making rash promises as to what it will be like in your wonderful homeland.

Missionaries who are returning "home" for the first time often succumb to the temptation to ship many things back to America. Stifle those urges! With today's cost of freight and postage it is impractical to ship heavy household items.

The people in American churches are usually very willing to help you if you let them know your basic needs for short-term housekeeping. Realize that your home there will be more temporary than your overseas home. You will probably be there a year or less. You will perhaps be traveling in deputation much of that time. The more simple you keep it, the easier it will be when it is time to go back overseas.

It is a great advantage to you now if you are returning to the same house after furlough. If someone will be "holding" your house for you, you won't need to dispose of furniture and other heavy items. Pack valuable or sentimental items that you wouldn't want to lose, in secure drums that can be locked and stored.

In many countries the last month of your time will perhaps be your busiest time in ministry. All those churches who have planned to ask you to speak for them will realize you are leaving and ask you to come, so you may be speaking much more often than you had during your term. Also friends and co-workers will want to have their last opportunity for a visit with you. Your last days will be very busy with farewelling. Because of this you should start preparing for your departure well in advance.

If you have to move out completely, start going through your things about three months before departure time. Dispose of what you won't need when you return.

The temptation is to deal first with the obvious—pictures on the wall, this sort of thing—and leave the things that are out of sight until the last minute. This is a mistake. Keep your home looking as comfortable as possible by leaving up pictures, curtains and other things that give it the "our home" imprint.

Start first to clear the unseen corners: drawers, medicine chest, trunks, cupboards and closets. You can do a thorough job of emptying these out-of-sight places without disrupting the settled appearance of your home. Don't forget to start early to clear your files, too. Dispose of any you no longer need.

It's great to have most of your dresser drawers and files empty and your closets and cupboards almost empty prior to your last week in the house. If you have gradually cleared your house of all the things that are out-of-sight, you can quickly clear the rest at departure time.

At least two months before you leave advise everyone who should know the dates of your impending departure: mission officials, local church officials, your children's teachers, immigration officials. Get copies of your children's school records or arrange for transcripts to be mailed. Get health records for all the family from your doctors.

Last of all, take down the pictures and personal items that make your house "homey." Save a few things that are special to you or your children. Take them with you or store them safely so you will have them on your return.

Plan to move out of rented quarters a week before departure. That gives you time to close all utility bills, phone bills, grocery bills, bank accounts, etc. It also gives you time for farewells! I think our record was ten different farewells when we left the Philippines.

If it's available where you live, it's helpful to get an international driving license before you leave. Then you can drive in most countries you go through. You can use it in America until you establish a residence.

In many countries everything you ship must be cleared by customs. In some places officials will come to your house to inspect, clear and seal your shipment. This saves you time later. Immigration officials will tell you what clearances you need. They may include a police clearance, income tax clearance, customs clearance, etc. These clearances can take a few days to a month or more to finalize. Don't delay too long or you will add frustration and confusion to your family's last days before departure. Plan for shipped items to arrive after you do, so you can avoid the high cost storage on the other end.

Be sure that you advise everyone in the homeland of your impending arrival. Tell the relatives, your church officials, your mission officials, and your home church so that all of them will know when you are returning. This does not mean that you should expect a royal welcome, but they should at least be informed of your arrival.

If you have kept some American money, teach your children the names and value of each coin while you are on the way home. If you don't have the cash, tell them about it, then show them the coins as soon as you get some. Shortly after she reached America my friend's little 7-year-old was humiliated by a scornful, "Dummy! don't you even know what a dime is?!"

Americans who have established a home overseas and will be returning overseas to live are classified as "non-residents" when they go through customs on re-entry to America for home leave (furlough).

This is very important to you. People who maintain their home in America and go abroad for travel or business are classified as "returning residents." The customs charges are vastly different for residents and non-residents. Many missionaries are not aware of this difference. They equate "residence" with "citizenship". Since they are American citizens they feel they should, on their customs form, mark themselves as residents. Residents are not allowed to bring in very many things, but non-residents are allowed to bring into America, duty free, all their personal belongings. These are personal belongings that are for your own use. They are strictly not for sale and must not be sold for at least a year. If you have established a home outside of America and have not maintained a home in America, be sure you re-enter as a "non-resident."

If you go into America at the large ports such as Honolulu or New York there will be different customs lines for residents and non-residents. The non-resident line usually moves much faster! Returning residents must make a written declaration of everything they have acquired since they left America. As a non-resident, you are only required to make on oral declaration of gifts you are bringing for others. I always list in a small notebook all the gifts I am bringing and their prices. I take receipts, too, but have never been asked to show them. I pack all the gift items in one bag. When the customs official asks if I am bringing gifts I show him my list of gifts and tell him which bag they are in. Officials always appreciate that. Usually they do not even bother to look at the gifts. They will look in a suitcase because they are required to check one. In going through customs seven times in three different ports in America I have always been treated with great courtesy and consideration. When you know what you should do, and do it right, the customs official appreciates your helpfulness and is in turn helpful to you.

Unless the laws are changed after this book is written, you do not need a written list of everything for customs. However, you should have a complete list of what is in your bags, for compensation in the event they are lost or damaged in transit.

If you have been away three years or more you will probably suffer some re-entry shock on your return. Things you have forgotten will stun you: the beautiful greenery if you return to the west coast from an arid country; the exhilarating dry air if you return to the southwest from a jungle region. On the other hand, you may be shocked by things you never noticed before. If you have worked in an underdeveloped area, the wasteful affluence you now see will worry you. People will appear to be too materialistic. You may even develop a hostile attitude about the life-style of family and friends. Avoid criticism as carefully now as you did four years ago in your host country. Remember, you are the one who is different!

If you have been living in an area where there is only slow travel you will be frightened by the fast moving vehicles and the freeways of America. This takes some adjustment.

If you have been struggling painfully in a "planting" ministry and return to a thriving church you will bask in the blessing. If you have been part of a "harvest team" in an area of great revival, you may feel that your home church is spiritually dead! Can you bless them?

If you've been quite removed from Western society you may feel very dowdy and out of style. You would be wise to ask someone (a relative, pastor's wife or some close friend who has a good sense of fashion) to shop with you the first time. You may still be thinking of what was fashionable four years ago and buy the wrong clothes.

When we first went overseas the most fashionable stockings were very sheer, with a black seam down the back. In the hot tropics I didn't wear hose for four years. I only saw someone with stockings on twice, and that was at the airport. I carefully hoarded my beautiful stockings in tupperwear for a stylish return.

We arrived by ship in New York City. As I hurried around the city taking care of details—picking up mail at American Express, maps at AAA, etc. I began to sense that something was wrong. Then it hit me! I was the only woman on the street with black seams . . . with *any* seams! Seamless stockings had arrived and I hadn't even heard!

When you shop for your new clothes it is better to just buy one good outfit than to try to get a lot of clothes that are cheaper. You will feel better in one good outfit. You will possibly be traveling from church to church for deputational ministry and will not need an abundance of clothes. After you are there a few months you'll feel more secure shopping. Most people are simply overwhelmed by the abundance of everything in the beginning.

If you have worked in a country where you have servants you must prepare for no servants on return to America. Of course there are servants: beautiful appliances and helpful people (school teacher, park employees, street cleaners, garbage collectors, librarians, mailmen) who do much of the work your servants did overseas. But there will be no one to help with household tasks. This is something that the family should prepare for long before leaving. The children should be taught to make their beds, clean their rooms, hang their clothes, and share in household chores. If you live in a country where you're required to have servants, it may not be easy to do this. The servants may feel that you're displeased with them or that it's not appropriate for the children to do it. But at least for a couple of months before you go require the children to do these things so that they are in the habit of doing them before they have to make the other big adjustments of re-entry in their Western culture.

When you settle in a home establish an equitable division of the house and yard chores. Very often when a missionary couple are on home leave the the wife has as much responsibility in ministry as the husband, because she will be called upon to speak for women's groups, young people's groups and children's groups. She may be speaking more than the husband, but to different kinds of groups. Also the wife may be furthering her training, to the same capacity that the husband is. In this case the husband can share in the chores that are a necessary part of life during the time they are at home, so the whole family can enjoy some leisure time together. If you decide the work distribution together in family discussion you can avoid the dissatisfaction and conflict that arise when one or two family members have to assume the entire servant load.

If your children have studied at home or in a small school their entry to a large public school can be frightening. By all means plan your arrival to give them some adjustment time in America before school starts. On the first day of school there will be other "new kids" so they won't stand out like a mango in a basket of peaches. Even so, your child may be the only one in a thousand who knows nothing about the system: lockers (one boy carried all his things for months rather than admit he didn't know how to use a combination lock); showers after P.E. (with 35 strangers—horrors!); paper rules (late slips, absentee notes, pink slips, white slips, yellow slips, etc. etc.). When you've attended a small school where everyone knows everyone's business the bureaucracy of a large impersonal school is overwhelming.

If you've been remote from American influence, the American life-style can be puzzling to your children. Some things they'll adore: grandparents, soft ice cream, hamburgers, pizza, TV (ours watched the *test pattern* the first day back). Some attitudes they'll question: strong sibling rivalry, rough language, disrespect to elders and teachers, slang expressions new to them.

Our daughter went to an American school the first time in fourth grade. The first two months she often came home with questions. "Mamma, my friend doesn't want her little sister to go trick-or-treating with us. Why wouldn't she?" (When your little brother is your only American playmate you want him around!) "Mamma, what does . . . . . mean?" (Oh, oh, another new four-letter word).

Perhaps the hardest thing on your teens will be when others treat them as "haloed": "Don't say that in front of a missionary's kid!" Some teens go to great lengths to keep it secret that they are missionary kids, because other teens (even church kids) will not accept them as one of the group. Some can handle it very well, others have to be outlandish to prove they are "normal".

When you're feeling a little shaken by differences on your first return, remember that your children have a much greater adjustment than you do. Pray for them and help them as you can. If you have lived where your children attend an American school, with students arriving regularly from North America, the adjustment will be much easier. They will be up-to-date on the "in" things: clothes, life-style, and new "slanguage."

At the last missionary conference I attended, two different missionary men asked me, "Why don't they ever tell you about culture shock your second term? It's harder than the first!"

To each I replied, "It will be in my book." It's true that your first return to your mission assignment is a big adjustment, especially if you have been gone a year or more. My theory is that the longer you are away the more you idealize the place you've left. While you're on furlough you idealize your mission situation just as you did your homeland during your first term.

If you spend your furlough in deputation (many missionaries conduct more than a hundred missionary services) you often relate the victories you have experienced overseas. Gradually the battles, loneliness and tears recede to dim memory. You return full of vigor and enthusiasm.

There are few experiences more thrilling than returning to a church you have established, seeing those "babes in Christ" now maturing and taking leadership in ministry to others. The first days are exciting. Then the problems (that never really left, only receded) begin to appear. Oh! You've been "home" and "back home" and you still haven't "returned to Paradise."

You arrive full of fervor for a new assignment that has been beautifully worked out (on paper) and approved all around. You set it in motion and guess what! Humans enter the scene. Someone doesn't like your idea. Or the finances run out. The beautiful balloon you carried around on deputation has burst. Pick up the pieces and carry on. All is not lost. Reality has just replaced dreams.

One mission chairman told me the attrition rate in their mission is highest early in the second term. He surmised that the comparison the missionary sees with his life situation and the life-style of his peers, in the homeland he's just visited, propels him back to his own country.

I think the contrast between reality and your dreams could be a major factor. Perhaps some who leave were "called to be a returned missionary" and have already fulfilled their vision!

At any rate, knowing that your second term is a sensitive time should help you to hold steady. Your children will usually settle in happily, relieved to be back to their "own" school or house. Even if you've changed locations, they'll probably be happier back in a more constant way of life than they were tramping around on furlough. Settle in! Your last big departure/arrival, thrill/adjustment is over. From here on you're a veteran!

More Learning Experiences

1. From the Reading List books, or other books, read 50 pages on the subject in this unit that interests you most.

2. Prepare an oral or written book review of one of the books on the Reading List on the subject of culture adjustment or the single missionary.

3. Interview a foreign national about cultural differences between your country and his country. Ask about holidays, marriage customs, gift-giving, family relationships, time concepts, and employer-employee relationships. Ask him to identify American customs that would be misunderstood by the people of his country.

4. To minister in a foreign country you need to separate what is cultural from what is Biblical in your standards. On the following subjects determine which of your ideas are Biblical (quote references) and which are inherited cultural patterns:
    a. Local church government
    b. Marriage ceremonies
    c. Religious celebrations (Easter, Christmas)
    d. Family roles
    e. Selection of a marriage partner
    f. Work standards

5. Ask a visiting missionary what cultural adjustments he had to make in order to fit into the country of his ministry. Ask which American customs would be offensive in that country.

PART III
Train Up a Child

12. Who Is "Old Glory"?

When you take your family to live in a foreign country be aware of the need to teach your children respect for two nations: the land where you live and the land of your citizenship.

You can best teach your children to respect the country you live in by always demonstrating that respect yourself. There may be aspects of life in the country that you regret: the political system may be oppressive; economic conditions may be discouraging; or the religious outlook may be bleak. Nevertheless, it is the place where you have chosen to live with your family. Your children will absorb your negative feelings if you continually disparage situations within the country. Guard against this.

Learn to understand the values of the country. Then you can show understanding and appreciation for positive aspects of the society. You can find attitudes and values to be thankful for and happy with, wherever you live. In your conversation at home express your appreciation for the good things in the community. Always demonstrate respect for both the nation and the people.

Of course you need to keep a sense of proportion and reality. Just as in your native country, you would not approve unscriptural practices even though they are acceptable in the society. For you should first of all teach your children to respect, obey and honor God's commands. What you must guard against, though, is the temptation to criticize or belittle situations in society that you dislike just because they are different from your own background experience. Show your children how to respect and honor the country and it will be easy for them to follow your counsel and example.

On the other hand, if your children have lived overseas from an early age, you will need to impart to them a knowledge of and respect for the land of your citizenship. Most Americans are quite proud of their democratic heritage. They do not stop to consider the source of their patriotism. Through all their growing up years they have imbibed these attitudes and feelings from teachers, preachers, formal citizenship studies, television, political campaigns, songs, stories, and a hundred informal influences.

Removed from most of these influences you grew up with, your children will not have the same appreciation for America that you have. You must act to instill in them appreciation for the far-removed land of their citizenship.

One solution is for parents to make use of celebrative days and events to explain to their children their American history and heritage. Make July 4th a special family day by having a picnic or some similar family activity. The children can on this day be told the stories of American history.

Other opportunities include Thanksgiving and President's Day. Don't let these special national days slip by unmarked in your family.

The American presidential elections are a good opportunity to explain how the American political system works. If it is possible where you live, be sure to have at least one American news magazine coming in to your home for your children to read as they are growing up. Discuss national events in the family, even though they seem far from your current life.

In addition, all children love to hear and read stories. Before the family goes overseas the parents should find books which have stories about important American events and people which the children would enjoy reading (George Washington, Johnny Applesced, the Pony Express, etc.).

A potential crisis may develop as the child grows older and begins to identify strongly with the country where he lives. The problem here is not with the child but with a possible over-reaction by the parents. It is perfectly natural for a young child to identify with and support the country where he is growing up. This is especially true if most of the children's friends are nationals of the host country, who would have natural patriotic feelings toward their own country. Your young child will probably learn the national anthem of your host country and may even talk of wanting to become a soldier in their armed forces or a citizen of the country. These are all natural desires on the part of children to identify with their peers. The best response of parents is to realize that if you present America in a proper light in your home, as your child gets older he will also show an appreciation of his own American heritage.

Americans often make the statement that the United States is the greatest country in the world. Upon moving overseas you may be surprised to find how many people in other countries don't agree. It is a shock to Americans to realize that in most countries the people love their country just as much as we do. In some cases, more! Thus, it is very important that Christian missionary families learn to be more subtle about their patriotism. Not only are displays of the American flag potentially offensive, in many countries there are definite rules concerning the display of alien flags on their soil. And although it may warm your heart to gather around and sing the "Star Spangled Banner", don't do it in the presence of other nationals unless you include *their* national anthem as well.

As a missionary it is important to realize that you are to proclaim the Gospel of Jesus Christ. To do this, you may have to submerge your own patriotic fervor while in foreign countries so you can better reach those people for Christ. The fine line you must walk is that of avoiding public displays of patriotism, but at the same time, in the privacy of your home, instilling love for your distant country in your children.

If your children live in two or more different cultures in their formative years they will be more world-minded than you will ever be. Their hearts may stir at the sound of more than one anthem; more than one set of national colors will lift their spirits. But the stirring and lifting will not be as intense as that of the national-minded person's. If you are a national-minded parent, understand and respect your children's world-view. When you took them overseas, you opened their mind to the world!

13. The Children's Hour

Some missionaries live in remote villages, their children constantly by their side. Others seem forever torn from their families by urban pressures or extensive travel. All need to consciously evaluate whether we wisely use the time available to us as "family time."

With the giving of the great commandment to love God with all our heart, soul and strength,[1] came advice of certain times of the day to use for teaching our children to also love and obey God. These times can become valuable family times when we make of them a "children's hour." The Bible here advises us to devote time to our children's learning when we go to bed and when we get up, when we sit at home and when we travel.

Many missionaries find the early morning time ideal for family devotions. Worshipping God together at home is a happy family time if everyone is really awake. For a family of natural "early risers" morning is a delightful time for devotions. If the children are only half-awake at breakfast, or a regular late-night work schedule makes it difficult for the parents to be alert in the early hours, family devotions should be at a later time. But if you have children leaving for school, you should share this early family time with them. A first grade teacher in an overseas American school once said to me, "You'd be surprised how many children leave for school without seeing their parents, who are still asleep . . . I mean missionary children!" Even very reliable household help cannot compensate for your attentive presence first thing in the morning. Don't let your children go off to face the day without your encouragement. Make at least a few moments of the early morning a "children's hour."

Whether your family devotions are early in the day or later they will be happiest and most effective if everyone actively participates. Sing songs the children enjoy. Read Bible portions suitable to the children's age. One missionary family read through Hurlbut's large Story Book of the Bible twice while their children were small.

Minister fathers need to avoid using family devotions as a preaching time. One woman (an MK) told me that if anything would have turned her against God it would have been their family devotions "because Dad always used it as a chance to 'get after' us kids." Real worship should be the goal of this children's hour.

Let the children have their turns at leading in family prayer. One missionary father pointed out that it is good to let the child's prayer "stand alone." He said, "If father or mother always feels compelled to pray after the child prays, the child gets the message that his prayer is not strong enough to get the family through the day."

A missionary mother and her visiting daughter, now grown, were at a prayer meeting where people were asked to pray spontaneously. When the daughter prayed her mother realized with a shock that she had not heard her daughter pray aloud since she'd heard her "little girl" bed-time prayers. Even though they'd had family devotions every day!

A home we visited more than 20 years ago had such a warm family time just before the children's bedtime that the memory still evokes happiness. We were three couples visiting after a year's separation. At one point the father invited us to worship with them before their three children (8, 9 and 10 years old) went to bed. We sang some lilting praise choruses, the father read from the Bible, then gave a brief application of the Word to daily living. Following this the children and we adults each shared one thing for which we were thankful. After prayer the children quite happily went off to bed as we continued to visit. Even if bedtime is not your devotion time, it should be a prime contender for a regular children's hour.

After struggling with the tug-of-war bedtime scene for a year or more I learned that devoting 30 minutes to a peaceful children's hour just before bedtime eliminated both the tugs and the war! Once I overheard our children talking in the next room. The 7-year old asked, "If you had to live with just mommy or daddy alone, which would you want to live with?" After a long pause, the 4-year old answered, "Well . . . I don't know . . . daddy plays with us . . . and mommy reads to us!"

Our individual contributions most important in his young eyes were two family times that had naturally evolved in our schedule. While I cooked dinner their daddy played rough and tumble games with them for a few minutes. Then at bedtime I spent about 30 minutes giving them my full attention: bathing, reading stories, getting drinks, answering questions, hearing prayers, and finally, "tucking in." This family time was early enough so they would be in bed before I had to go out for church or other activities. We frequently had guests in the home, but I always gave the children their full "family time." The reward was a peaceful happy bedtime for them and an interruption-free evening for work or relaxation for my husband and me.

Another good children's hour is when you sit together at meal time. It is perhaps the easiest time for everyone to get together on a regular basis. It is a good time to share the hopes and needs of your ministry with your family. You can also acquaint the children with distant relatives and churches in your "sending country" by sharing letters from them. It is a good time for the children to share their dreams or to tell the parents about their activities at school or play.

It is not a good time for correction or punishment. True, table manners must be taught. But this can be done quietly, with only the parent who first notices the need for correction or instruction giving it. It need not become a family issue with both parents, and perhaps older brothers or sisters joining in to overwhelm the young offender.

When the family is at home together, either at meals or "each doing his own thing," if love, respect and giving are freely shared it is a strengthening children's hour.

Few families travel more than missionaries. Travel can be looked on as an endurance test or obstacle course. Or it can be wisely used as a children's hour. One missionary mother entertained her children by telling them stories during long auto trips. Once when her storybook memories failed she launched into some true tales from her own childhood. From then on, until the children left for college, on every long trip the request came, "Tell us more, Mom, about what you did when you were young. You, too, Dad." Thus, the childhoods of the two generations were linked. The parents became real people in their children's eyes. A lasting bond was forged.

Other families enjoy singing or playing games as they travel. As the children reach their teens it is a good time for serious conversation about the great questions of life.

One of the delightful results of taking care to establish a children's hour is that we can readily use these family times to teach our children God's Word. The best teaching is done in unplanned sessions as we respond with answers from the Bible to their urgent questions or needs. Of course, we need to be prepared for the "follow up teaching" that results from these informal Bible lessons. I remember one rather hilarious outcome of my earnest attempts to teach my son to quit hitting his sister.

Following the advice in Deuteronomy 6:7, I coupled my behavior teaching with scripture. He was about 7 years old when I first enjoined him to "do to your sister what you would want her to do to you."[2] His quick answer, "I *am* doing what she wants to do to me!"

Much patient explaining helped him to understand the Golden Rule and it held the hitting in check very well until he was about 9. Then one day he came home from school with questions about a religion he had just encountered for the first time. I explained that the religion was based on the Bible, but it overemphasized one verse of scripture without the balanced teaching of the rest of the Bible. This was followed by my little lecture on the importance of finding the balance in the Bible for our beliefs and behavior.

All went well for about a month. Then one day he roared out of his room exulting, "Mom! I found the balance! I found the balance!"

To my puzzled "What?" he explained, "You know how you're always telling me, 'Do to others what you want them to do to you'? Well, here's the balance: 'An eye for an eye, a tooth for a tooth, . . . wound for wound, stripe for stripe'!"

Be prepared!

Travel time can relate to necessary travel for ministry or a time planned for family recreation. When you are settled it is wise to have a regular time for recreation with the children. When they are toddlers some play time every day with mom and dad, together or separately, is valuable growing experience.

If the parents schedule is very tight, a set time for recreation once a week gives the children something to look forward to all week. One father has his three sons list on separate slips of paper the things they like to do with him (play ball, swim, hike, just talk, etc.). Each Friday after school and office hours Dad takes one suggestion from the "family time" box and they all enjoy that day's fun together. When the ideas have all been used they start over. As the boys mature the plans change, but they always know that on Friday afternoon their wishes come first with their busy dad. Busy missionary fathers, your children don't need a lot of your time, but they do want to know that there is a time when you will put them first. Schedule a time for your children, and keep that time for them.

Most American churches have excellent programs for training children in the Word of God: sunday school, Neighborhood Bible clubs, Missionettes (for girls), Royal Rangers (for boys) Christian Cadets, children's church, etc.

When parents take school-age children overseas for the first time they may find no Bible study programs available for them in their own language. If there is a thriving church they can fit into the children's programs as soon as they learn the language. Until then you must provide the regular Bible training.

You will be wise to take with you a complete set of Sunday school lessons and students' supplies. I taught my children Sunday school on shipboard from the first Sunday after we sailed from America, and for many years overseas. After they knew the local dialect well enough to attend a Sunday school class in the local church, we continued to have "Sunday school" in English at home on Wednesdays! Both on shipboard and overseas, there were always other English-speaking children who joined our classes. Through these classes not only did our own children receive steady formal training in the Word, but also other children and their parents came to know Christ.

If there are any other missionaries in your area, perhaps you can start a Bible study hour for the children together, with co-operative teaching from the parents.

One missionary mother told me her daughters had started "missionettes" in the states. This program for girls incorporates Bible study with many other good learning experiences. When they came overseas she brought the entire program with her. Their "Missionette meeting" once a week (just the two girls and their mother) became a delightful children's hour for them.

The most important help that you can give to your child is a sure foundation in the Word of God and in the basic tenets of Christianity. The time comes when he has to be on his own. It comes much sooner for some than for others. Some children go away to boarding school as early as 7 and 8 years old. Many go away to boarding school for high school. Others are left in their home country during their high school years. The basis that you give them in the home, from their earliest years until they leave you, is the strongest influence they will ever receive toward a vital Christian life.

The Bible says, "Train a child in the way he should go, and when he is old he will not turn from it."[4] Giving time to your children is part of that training. When you make the children's hour an inviolate part of your schedule you say to your child, "I love you and you are important to me."

14. The International School of WHAT?!

When we have taught seminars on "the missionary family" to prospective missionary candidates in America 80 percent of their written questions asked about schooling for missionary children. Certainly this is one of the first problems that a missionary faces on taking his children overseas.

Parents cannot continue in their work happily unless they are convinced that they are doing the best for their children. School difficulties can cause serious family problems, or even result in the parents giving up their missionary career, but this is rare indeed.

There are more options in the questions of schooling than most people realize. Your children's schooling need not be a major factor in your decision of where or when to answer the Lord's call for missionary service. You can trust the Lord to provide for the education of the children He has given you, on the field to which He has called you. You have a choice between educating your children at home or sending them to school away from home. In each of these choices there are also alternatives.

Our children both graduated from the International School of Kuala Lumpur. The title of this chapter is the unvarying response of anyone who asks them where they went to high school. If your children go to Nairobi or Kadaikanal they will get the same response!

As in Kuala Lumpur, in many countries there are American schools or international schools, which often follow an American system of education. Usually these schools are academically excellent and almost always superior to American public schools. A typical international school will have many teachers who have done extensive post-graduate work and who are highly skilled professionals. Often the students represent many different countries and cultures. This exposure will broaden your children's world view. Since their classmates are often the children of highly educated and skilled people, your children will tend to take a more serious look at academic work, college, and professional careers.

There are also disadvantages to an international school. Since they are usually college prep schools, there may be no vocational training offered. If your child is a poor student or has little aptitude for academic work he may feel lost in a school of students preparing to go to top-notch colleges.

Another problem which often occurs is that most families who send their children to an international school will be quite wealthy, especially when compared to the average missionary. It is important that parents of missionary kids in international schools speak honestly to their children about their financial limitations and help the child to understand that having less money is not to be deplored. It is equally important that the parent keeps the child from developing a belligerent "we poor against you rich" attitude in the school. One of the most tiring things for others to hear is the continual whining of someone about his alleged poverty. Qualities, such as honesty and decency, and talents still count far more than dollars. This is a good lesson for MK's to learn and to teach their schoolmates.

Often a problem arises because the life style of these international school students and their parents is quite different from your associates in the United States. Social drinking is common and there is a great deal of emphasis on such activities as nightclubs and cocktail parties. It is important that any parents who send their children to an international school have an open relationship with their children which includes talks about the kind of social standard the parents expect their children to maintain.

In a few instances where a missionary lives near a U.S. military installation their children are allowed to enroll in a school for military dependents. The school will be much like an American public school, except that both students and faculty are more transient, with few remaining more than two years.

Many parents, who find themselves in a place where there is no acceptable American or international school, choose to teach their children by means of a correspondence school. There are basically two approaches to having a correspondence school for one's children. The most common is for one of the parents, almost always the wife, to teach the children.

Another approach is to find a tutor to teach your children. If a good tutor can be found this is probably better than having one of the parents teach the student. One advantage is that if the tutor is a national he can teach the child about the customs and way of life of the country, in addition to his school subjects. If the tutor is from the United States he can provide a link to America which will often make things easier on the MK when he returns to the United States.

Of course, one advantage to using a tutor is that the parents are freed to do full-time missionary work. The family is also relieved of the strain which can come when the normal parent-child relationship is complicated by teacher-student roles.

If you use a tutor, be careful that you never undermine the tutor's authority with the student. It would be impossible for a tutor to develop any kind of good teaching environment if the parents constantly discuss his bad traits in front of the child. Determine if the tutor is the best available, then keep your doubts to yourself. Anything else is unfair to everyone.

In some locations, if you want to keep your children at home, your only choice is to teach them yourself. I taught my children five years and treasure the experience. The privilege of sharing so many learning experiences with your child is rare in today's splintered society. If you have this opportunity approach it with positive excitement. Learning can be fun!

Face any negative factors and deal with them realistically. Recognize that the schooling will take 2 to 4 hours of your time every day. Set the time aside. Don't try to sandwich it in among other jobs or you and your child will be continually frustrated. From kindergarten to grade two, give your total attention. As the child gets older he will require less of your time. You will be able to read, write, sew or study while he studies. But it is a good idea to stay in the classroom with him throughout the primary grades.

Lack of teacher training or experience need not intimidate you. Correspondence courses are planned for individual study without a trained teacher's help. If your course has the option of sending lessons to a school for regular reports, by all means do so. Your child will eagerly work for a good report from his "teacher" at the school. The grades and reports from the school will also be his only way of seeing how he compares with other correspondence students. Be aware that correspondence schools usually grade more strictly than an American public school does.

Before you go overseas ask to see the I.Q. and Achievement Test evaluations of your school children. Even in schools where these scores are not shared with parents, the counselor will usually give you the information when you explain that you will be teaching the child the next four years. If your children are preschoolers you may be able to have them tested at a university or teacher's college. Ask your local public health services if testing is available.

Although this testing is not required, it will help you to know what standard of work to expect from your child. The worst negative factor for the parent teaching his own child is the parent's tendency to demand perfection. I have seen a parent make a child do the same lesson over and over, so he would get an A, when the child should not be expected to do above C level work. Follow the guidance in the course, encourage your child in his work, but do not be too critical or put undue pressure on him to excel.

Whether you teach your own child or use a tutor it will help to establish a "real school" atmosphere if you:

(1) keep regular hours, starting at a set time every day
(2) set up a special "school room", even if it's a corner of the bedroom, living room, or porch, with desk, bookcase, chalkboard, etc.
(3) establish the teacher/student relationship from the beginning
(4) allow only emergency interruptions: a very unusual visitor; special holidays; fire, earthquake or typhoon.

There are several things which can be done to enhance a correspondence school education. You can often hire someone to teach a special subject, such as music, Latin, or a modern language. Your child may take up a local sport, such as soccer, sepak takraw, top-spinning, kite-flying, or tae kwon do. Many countries have Boy Scout and Girl Scout programs your child can join.

Often several missionaries who have children studying by correspondence will have them meet in a common classroom so that only one teacher is required to supervise them. This is also good because it helps to add a classroom feeling. You may be able to pool resources with missionaries and other expatriates in the area to establish a co-operative school. A regular classroom is established by the parents. Then a professional teacher is hired to supervise the students in their correspondence work. The students may then enjoy group activities such as singing, sports, field trips, and recreational activities. Many international schools started as co-operative schools. As more students joined they expanded to regular schools.

A big advantage of correspondence study is that the student doesn't miss anything in the curriculum when he is ill or has to travel. Also, he learns good work habits. He will develop excellent writing abilities much earlier than public school students do.

Both of our children wrote interesting little "books" of about 15 pages in second grade. When our daughter went to public school in America for the first time in fourth grade she was astonished that they were only learning to write paragraphs. When she again attended school in America in 9th grade her English teacher called to talk to me because he thought someone was writing her compositions for her. I assured him that no one had even read them before he did. He said they were like good college writing. That was the result of four years of correspondence study and an excellent English teacher in the small American school where she took 5th-to-8th grade studies.

The intimacy of shared experiences and the joy of seeing your child learn far outweigh the negative aspects of teaching your own child. Count your blessings!

There is a third option which may work out well in many cases and this is sending your children to the local national schools. This is especially worth investigating in any of the countries where the schools are taught in English. One big advantage of this option is that the child learns a lot about the local culture and life style. It also provides them with an active social life with the national people, something which is often appreciated by the local church.

In many of the former British colonies the educational system is good, with high standards. Many of these schools actually are much harder and teach a higher level than the public schools in America. This is because education is neither free nor compulsory, so only the hard-working students with scholastic aptitude are in school, especially in high schools. Before enrolling your child in a local school be sure to check with your state board of education in America to see if any additional courses would be needed by your children for their diplomas to be accepted in your state. Often they can take a course in American History and American Government by correspondence to fulfill these requirements. As the child gets older, contact the colleges he is interested in to see if they would have any additional requirements.

When the local schools are not in English the problem is more complex. Some missionary parents choose to send their children to the local school anyway. As a result these children develop extensive skills in other languages which often help them in later life. After our children were fluent in the local language, we sent them half-day to the local school in primary grades, then taught them their English correspondence studies at home in the afternoon. It worked very well for us.

Many parents send their children to a mission-run boarding school, either in the same country or in a neighboring country. There are many definite advantages in doing so. Academically, your children will study under professional teachers who are hand-picked for their ability to deal with students in a boarding situation. Your children will also have the benefit of classroom discussion and interaction with fellow students. At such a school they would have access to a library, labs and workshops. In addition there would be proper testing for progress and knowledge. Not only would the classroom competition provide incentive to work, but college scholarships are much easier to obtain for graduates of recognized schools.

There are many social benefits for children at a mission boarding school. Children who attend boarding school are often quite mature because they learn at an early age how to obey rules, handle responsibility, and get along with others. In addition the older students learn to help care for younger students. There is, of course, the social benefit of having a large peer group with which to develop relationships. Many lasting friendships are formed. Also important is the opportunity to participate in group activities such as sports, dramas, and musical groups. Since most mission groups are traditionally music-oriented, the music departments at these schools are often far superior to those of other schools.

There are also many spiritual benefits to a missionary school. In addition to the Bible studies given as part of the academic curriculum of the school, there are regular chapel services.

In most schools the students have opportunities to minister through evangelism. Active church participation is encouraged. One benefit which is often overlooked is that of a student having Christian teachers. Children usually imitate their teachers, either consciously or not, and it is a great benefit to have teachers who would be good Christian examples to children.

One benefit to the parents is that if their children are away in a boarding school they are freed for full-time missionary service. This is perhaps more true of the missionary wife than the husband. With no children at home she can concentrate on ministry. The parents are also able to take trips of great length into areas where they could never have ventured if they had children at home that needed to be cared for. However, your decision to send your children to boarding school should be based on what is best for the children, not on the freedom it will give you.

There is one real objection to sending children to boarding schools. That is the separation of the children from their parents. Many families feel that this single factor outweighs all of the possible benefits, especially when the children are small. It is certainly true that some missionary children have developed problems that can be traced to a traumatic separation from their parents at an early age.

Each family needs to carefully weigh the pluses and minuses for themselves. Some of the most closely knit families are those where the children are separated from their families by a boarding school, because the time that the children spend with the parents during vacations is maximized as "family time".

Many families reach a compromise by teaching their children when they are in their early formative years. Then from about sixth grade, or their teen years they go to boarding school to gain the social interaction which is so important in the development of a teenager.

Parents sometimes choose to leave their children in the United States, either living with friends of relatives or in a boarding school in America. The type of arrangement seldom seems to work out as well and produces some very unhappy teen-agers. The friend or aunt or uncle who seemed so pleasant to visit for a weekend while on furlough can be revealed as a different person during the course of a year's stay. Also, the child is virtually left with no real parent-figure, since friends and relatives seldom feel free to exercise the disciplinary authority role over someone else's child. The modern public school system certainly would not provide the young boy or girl the responsible figure that professional teachers, counselors, and dorm-parents would in a boarding school situation.

Most boarding schools in America are of the prep-school type. Although they are often academically excellent they may teach a decidedly non-Christian value system which the parent 10,000 miles away has no chance of countering.

Christian boarding schools in America might better meet your needs. But the students whose parents are two continents away have adjustment problems unknown to those who can call or visit their parents whenever the need arises.

When you have investigated all the possible choices and prayerfully decided which one is best for your child, stick with it without complaining. Give your child a chance to learn without being distracted by your negative thoughts and comments. Don't forget, both a good and a bad education can be obtained almost anywhere. Let the whole family have their say in the decision and then give it a fair trial.

Useful Addresses

General Information:
Department of Defense Overseas Dependents Schools, Department of Defense, Washington D.C. 20301

Maher, A., ed. *Schools Abroad of Interest to Americans,* Porter Sargent, 11 Beacon Street, Boston, Massachusetts 02108. 1975

Office of Overseas Schools, Department of State, Washington D.C. 20520

Kindergarten to Eighth Grade:
Calvert School, Tuscany Road, Balitmore, Md. 21210

International Institute, P.O. Box 66053, Chicago, Ill. 60666

Kindergarten though High School (Christian Viewpoint):
Alpha-Omega Publications, P.O. Box 3153, Tempe, Arizona 85281

Missionary Accelerated Christian Education, P.O. Box 16161, Mobile, Alabama 36616

High School:
Department of Correspondence Instruction, University of California Berkeley, Calif. 94720

Extension Division, University of Nebraska, Lincoln, Neb. 68503

Also check with your own state university or teacher's college for information on available correspondence studies or enrichment courses.

15. Roots and Wings

Last Christmas our daughter sent us a stitchery wall hanging she made for us. The scene shows a boy and girl sitting by the gnarled roots of a strong old tree. They are watching blue birds fly off in the distance. The motto says: "There are only two lasting things we can give our children . . . one is roots, the other wings." In her card she wrote, "You've endowed me with strong, healthy roots in all areas of my life and given wings to test them and live my own life!"

Joy's roommate her first three years in college had grown up in one house and had the same room all her life. It is still her room when she and her husband visit home! To her, Joy's life seemed rootless, without a home to return to. The true roots, though, are not the house, but the family. Even if your children grow up in several different continents, a warm family relationship gives them strength to develop on their own.

Missionaries need to start early to help their children develop independence. They may need to fly on much younger wings than their stateside peers do. In chapter five we wrote about teaching your children to handle their own travel papers. Do this by the time they are in school.

Avoid overprotection of your children. One missionary told me, "No wonder it was a shock for Jane to go home to colllege! We never ever allowed her to ride the bus or go to town alone here. Then we sent her off to travel through three countries and settle in the States alone. What a pity that we didn't give her some independence earlier!"

Start early to encourage your child to make decisions about, and care for, his personal needs: hair cuts and styles, clothing purchases and upkeep, health care, dietary habits, recreation schedules, sleep schedules, and study habits.

From their pre-school years give your children a realistic allowance and teach them to live within their budget. Let them know exactly what their allowance must cover and don't bail them out when they overspend on luxuries. They will quickly learn if you let them! The child who can always call on Mom or Dad for anything he wants has difficulty coping with finances on his own.

In some missions, church support groups may be very generous with gifts to a missionary child. Teach your child to be appreciative of these added blessings. Also help him to know that these are "extras" and not something he can always expect. Teach him to be a "giver", as well as a gracious "receiver".

As your child approaches the time when he must "leave the nest", do not burden him with your own dependence on him. Certainly, assure him that you will miss him. But let him see that you trust him to manage well on his own. A grieving mother or father puts a great weight on a child who is facing many other difficult adjustments when he leaves home for the first time. It is hard enough to say goodbye to a well-loved land and friends, without worrying about Mom and Dad's reaction.

When our daughter prepared to leave Malaysia to return to America for college she said to me, "I'm so glad that we moved from the Philippines to Malaysia for our third term. I think if I had spent three terms in one country, it would have been too hard to leave." This illustrates the depth with which your children may identify with the country where you're serving as a missionary.

Many missionaries do stay in one location for their entire

missionary career. Children who are born in that location, or spend most of their growing up years there, will feel much more at home there than they do in their parent's home country. They may choose to spend their life there if they find work there that they enjoy.

Missionaries often fail to be alert to the fact that their children will not have the same feelings of loyalty and "home" that the parents do for their native country. If this is pleasing to you it is not a problem. If, however, you want to be sure that your children have a choice between the two ways of life, you should take measures to keep them familiar with your home country. There are different ways you can do this: by talking about the home land; by taking a longer home leave as they grow older; or by making the decision to stay back in your home country for a few years with the child when he is in his late teens. You do need to be aware that if you keep a child in another country for all of his growing-up years, that may become more "his" country than the land of your own birth.

Along with this same consideration is the realization that your child will reach the age when it is normal to have boy-girl relationships, engagement and marriage. If they are living overseas it is quite possible that they will form these relationships with nationals of the country where they live. Or they might marry expatriates from countries other than your own country of citizenship. This is a situation that missionary parents need to face squarely. You need to explore your own feelings about it. If you choose to keep your children with you abroad during their late teens, ask yourself if you are ready to accept a possible choice of a local marriage partner.

If the parent is very strongly determined that the child should marry someone of his own citizenship, he should make arrangements for the child to be in that country during the years when it is natural for him to meet a life partner. In many countries where missionaries serve, there is a large expatriate community and many other young people of his own nationality. However, the Christian community might be quite small. You may prefer to have your children in a society where there will be more involvement with Christian young people.

Remember: you can give your children both roots and wings. Encourage and respect their growing independence. Face the "empty nest" years with cheerful courage and you will give them courage and strength.

16. Off To College

If your children have stayed with you in your country of ministry until they reach college age, they will probably be leaving to return to your home country for their university training. It is your responsibility as parents to ensure a good choice for his college training by familiarizing yourself with the requirements of colleges that are available to him. On your last home leave before your child will be ready for college, try to visit the universities or Bible colleges that he might be interested in attending. Let your child choose his own college and career, but make sure that you help him to know all the options that are available for him.

You should also investigate scholarship programs that are offered in America for training in the career of your child's choice. Check into available scholarship programs by contacting counselors at the high schools of your home leave area for this information. The information may not be available in your overseas school.

Many missionary children, because of their extra advantage of world travel and broader life-experience, come to college with better academic preparation than the average American high school student. The schools they attend abroad are college-preparatory schools rather than schools with many vocational subjects. The student has opportunity for a thorough grounding in languages, math, science and social studies. If he has studied by correspondence he has already learned to work well on his own. Due to these factors a large percentage of missionary children going home to college will be advanced in their academic knowledge. They may be able to test high on college board examinations and receive college credit for the knowledge they received in high school.

Encourage your children to take the college board examinations in order to advance to their proper college placement. A student who is required to take basic courses that cover information he already knows will become bored. He will not be challenged in his early college experience. He may become restless and get into difficulty, or want to leave school.

If your child is old enough to leave home, but does not want to attend college, respect his wishes. Some young people are more interested in working than studying. Some will decide to go to college after they work a year or two. Others may find a stimulating and satisfying job without college. Give them wings!

Though your child may be better prepared for college academically than the average American high school student, he can be light years away from his American peers socially. They are in step with each other because they have grown up together. They know all the "right" words, relationships, customs, styles, etc. He has to learn. Fast!!

In some instances children have lived most of their lives in areas that are drastically different from America and may be ill-prepared for adjustment to American life. One such case is those who live in a remote, primitive area where life is very simple. A student coming from such a background may be overwhelmed by the materialism of America, by the availability of everything, or by the life-style. Adjustment is difficult. Prepare your child in every way possible. Talk frankly with him so he knows what to expect when he reaches America.

I personally feel that if a child has been very protected, has lived in a remote area, and has not travelled on his own, it is advisable for one parent to accompany him home when he leaves for boarding school or college. Nevertheless, if this is not financially possible, your child is certainly old enough at college age to manage alone.

Another life situation that lends itself to a difficult adjustment is where a rigid class system requires that you have servants. In this case your child may have never been allowed to take care of himself in regard to housework, his clothes, etc. This can happen! As a foreigner you are forced to respect certain customs of behavior. However, you serve your child poorly if you do not teach him to care for all his own needs before he leaves for college. He should have experience doing his own laundry. He should know how to cook. A student who goes to college and does not know how to manage daily chores will quickly become a burden to his roommates. He will be scorned and avoided by his American peers.

It is extremely important that your child learn how to drive, because a car is a necessity in the American way of life, except in the large eastern cities. In many American locations, it is difficult to get a job or go many places without a car. Your college freshman doesn't need to own his own car, but he will be ridiculed if he doesn't know how to drive. Teach him how to drive before he goes to America. If the laws of your country do not permit him to drive on public roads, at least show him how to manage a car (start, stop, reverse, etc.) in your yard or garage. Teach him all you can about the care of a car.

It is helpful if your child can get some work experience before he starts to college. Before our daughter went home for college, Les wrote to the university to see if she could work there a few weeks before school started. They were happy to hire her in the office because August was when most of the staff wanted a vacation. This worked out very well for Joy. She got acquainted with staff members and learned her way around the college before the two thousand other students poured in. She liked the job so well that she kept it until she graduated. You might try this idea, too.

When your children leave for college be sure that you write to them regularly whether they write or not. Remember that they will be very busy. They will be adjusting to a new way of life. They will be with classmates, roommates or dormmates who probably will not be writing letters to anyone, so do not expect heavy correspondence from them. Do not resent it when you do not hear from them. But continue to write regularly to lend them your support.

If your child starts college while you are on furlough, or in your first year overseas, he faces a long separation from you. Some missions pay the fare for college children to visit their overseas home once during their college years. Just knowing they can go home once more relieves much of the stress of separation.

If your mission does not pay the fare for your children to come home, I strongly recommend that you plan to help them make the trip at least once. When our children were in college we told them if they could save the money to come home once we would pay their way back. Joy came after graduation. We had been on furlough during her sophomore year. David came at the end of his freshman year. They were fortunate that they could get a charter flight from Seattle to Hong Kong for $250 one way then. Some destinations cost much more. We made this offer to them to remove the strain of their feeling they were totally and forever cut off from their home.

More Learning Experiences
1. Invite one or more sons or daughters of missionaries to a question-and-answer session with your group. Learn what kind of schools they attended. Discuss the advantages and disadvantages of each kind of schooling. Think about how you can be prepared to choose and carry out the best schooling for your own children if you become a missionary.

2. Learn through interviews with missionaries or their sons or daughters the adjustments "MK's" face when they return to America. Discuss what can be done by church and college mission-interest groups to help the returning "MK" to avoid these problems.

3. Write to your church's state missions director to learn what "MK" will be coming to attend a high-school or college near you. Welcome

the student on arrival. Help him find a job if he needs one. Introduce him to a helpful returning student who can guide him through the first days at school.

4. Give an offering to help an MK returning form the tropics to buy a winter coat or sweater.

5. Arrange and pay for a telephone call from an MK in the states to his distant parents on their birthday or a special holiday.

PART IV

Divers Problems

17. Pesos, Rupees, Francs

The managing of family finances is an omnipresent part of missionary life. Recognize from the beginning that you are choosing a way of life that is not expected to bring you financial gain. Compared to your peers in America your income may seem quite penurious.

On the other hand, if you serve in a poorly developed country, you may be rich in goods compared to most of the people who live there. As a foreign "oddity" you may be invited to the homes of the few elite families and feted royally on occasion. With Paul you can say, "I know what it is to be in need, and I know what it is to have plenty."[1] Expect this disparity in your social contacts. Do not be duped into the fallacy that you should have the same life-style as the rich whom you contact overseas.

When our children were very small we were one of only four American families in a city of 150,000. They were invited to play with children who lived in some very elaborate homes, as well as those in the simple homes of our neighborhood.

One day I overheard 3-year-old David ask 7-year-old Joy, "How do people get rich?"

She responded, "You work real hard and make lots of money" . . . (a long pause) . . . "and you don't build *any* churches!!"

We had built a church where we pastored in America and were then building churches in some towns and villages near our city. She assumed that was where any extra money went. And she was right!

You may think you have made a commitment to a life without riches. But when you see other foreigners living very well, you may find yourself discontented with your financial state. You may begin to want things that are clearly beyond your means. You may even begin to wonder if you could do some "moonlighting" for extra cash. Beware!

Determine to live within your mission budget. Frankly discuss with the whole family the things you cannot afford. A certain food (such as cheese) that was a family basic in America may now be a luxury. You may have to give it up. Look around for good substitutes. In your new location a food you once considered expensive (such as bananas or avocados) may now be in abundant supply.

Former favorite pastimes may now be expensive. If your family were voracious readers of library books and periodicals you may be shocked to learn that you will now have to buy all your reading material, at much higher prices!

In countries where the standard of living is very high (as in Japan or Europe) clothing may cost much more than at home. On the other hand, in many tropical countries locally made clothes will be much cheaper than in America. Count your blessings and adjust to what is locally available.

Other expatriates will make frequent trips to their home country at government or company expense. Fares will be paid for their college-age children to come home for Christmas and summer vacations. Avoid comparing yourself to these people who are on a different economic scale.

If you can learn to live within your budget with praise and thanksgiving, you will eliminate a great source of friction, concern, and tears from your family life. One formula for living in the budget that I recommend is "Tithe 10 percent, save 10 percent, and spend the rest with thanksgiving and praise."[2] You may feel that your allowance does not allow you enough for saving. Remember that your mission pension program is savings. Social security payments to the government are also a help for the future. Money that is deducted by your mission from your salary, for your children's education, medical expenses, or retirement can also be counted as savings.

If your mission does not separate any savings from your salary, you can ask your bank to automatically transfer 10 percent of your salary into a savings account. If you never receive it you will not miss it! Then you will have a savings built up against emergencies, or for future needs. Certainly you will tithe your 10 percent! Then you will have approximately 80 percent of your salary to live on. Budget your family living and live within your means.

Another good guideline for living within your means: never borrow money for something that will depreciate in value. A home does not fall into this category. Our mission encourages missionaries to buy a house in the states before they go overseas if possible.

Finance experts say that owning a home is the best hedge against inflation.[3] If you already own a home, keep it and have a reputable real estate dealer handle the rentals while you are overseas. Even if you will not live in it again, its sale would give you a down payment on a home in another location later on. If you can live in it during succeeding furloughs, it will give your children some stateside roots.

You may need to borrow money for education, your's or your children's. But an education, properly used, will appreciate in value and enrich your life.

Do not borrow for luxuries. On the other hand, avoid being miserly. Enjoy what God provides for you. Know how to abound! If God sends, through one of his children, a special gift, treat the family to a special outing or buy a "want", not always only a "need".

Teach your children that God will provide you're needs and some of your "wants", as well. Teach them to be appreciative and to praise God for his blessings. In some missions, church support groups are generous with gifts. Teach your children to express their appreciation to anyone who sends them a gift. Also make them realize that each gift is special and not to be taken for granted. They must not grow up expecting to always be on the receiving end.

Live within your mission allowance and teach your children to budget their own allowance. If an extra personal offering comes your way, use it for the unexpected extra luxury or save it towards your home or retirement. Don't make the mistake of depending on extra gifts for ordinary daily living expenses. Give 10 percent, save 10 percent and spend the rest with thanksgiving and praise.

18. Help!

Before we went to our first appointment in an area where all the missionaries had servants we were told, "Don't call the people who work for you 'servants', but 'helpers'." The person speaking was interrupted by a snort of laughter from her son at the term "helper". He then proceeded to regale me with amusing tales of horror regarding the "help" people received, beginning with the incident when a missionary showed her new helper how to pluck a chicken, clean it, cut it up and cook it.

The next time chicken was on the menu the missionary returned from language school near noon. On entering the kitchen she heard wierd noises in the refrigerator. On investigation she found a nude live chicken protesting vigorously. When the missionary had demonstrated "how to prepare and cook a chicken" the week before, she'd skipped the all important first step! Because she didn't want to kill a chicken she'd had her husband do it before the "cooking lesson" began. A painful omission, for the chicken!

Thus I went, expecting my "Help!" to be a cry for assistance, or even deliverance! To my delight, in the thirteen years we lived where we had servants, my cry "Help!" usually indicated a positive "Praise the Lord! I have someone who capably and efficiently frees me from routine house and yard duties so I can devote my time to teaching and other ministries."

If your ministry is in a developing nation you may be faced for the first time with the opportunity, the privilege, or even the requirement of having servants in your home. This situation is rapidly changing. Increased employment opportunities for working people, inflation, and the rising standards of living have made a servant's wages too high for missionaries in much of the world. However, if you live in a land where there is high unemployment you may be considered selfish if you refuse to hire someone to help in your home.

You need to adjust to the situation in the country where you work. If you are expected to have servants you should accept that and live with it. You will find that you can certainly have problems, but you also can find it to be a great blessing to your ministry as you are freed to devote more time to activities in the mission.

One good reason why servants are required in some countries is the lack of security. You need someone in the house at all times to prohibit thievery. If you do not have a servant one family member will always be required to stay in the house, 24 hours of every day. If the house if left empty it's an open invitation to petty thieves to "help yourself to what you want".

The other major reason is to fit into the status the community accords you. You may find that even your servants will have servants to do their work and tend their children! If that is the way of life you need to adjust to it.

Living with servants is sometimes the greatest adjustment problem that Americans face when they go overseas. For a hundred years only very wealthy Americans have had housemaids, chauffeurs, or gardeners. The mind-set of the missionary rebels against being placed in that category. Some women who revel in the homemaker role feel that their greatest gift of ministry to their family is displaced when they have servants. If they have had few interests outside their home, they may deeply resent the "intrusion" into their role as cook or housekeeper.

Mothers of young children probably accept helpers in the home more readily than anyone else. Since babies and toddlers require 24-

hour supervision, it is a great help to have someone share in this care. Some mothers will not allow a helper to care for their children, but the helper relieves them of household chores so they are free to spend all their own spare time with the children. Other mothers turn over the total care of their children to helpers. Hopefully, you can avoid either of these extremes and work out a happy relationship with your child's "caretaker".

If you are in language study or another full-time occupation, you may need to leave the children with a caretaker for long hours. In this case, try to reserve for yourself the intimate care of your little ones during your hours at home; feeding, bathing, bed-time rituals, waking up time. While the children are napping or playing outside a caretaker can supervise them and give you time for your studies and work. If you share intimate hours daily with your child you needn't feel threatened that the helper will take over your "mother" role.

If you consistently put the children to bed at an early hour the helper can baby-sit while they sleep, allowing you to attend evening functions without disrupting the children's rest. Some American families are not aware that people of many countries do not expect children to attend evening social functions to which the parents are invited. Young missionary families who have always taken their children when invited out for dinner in America are sometimes deeply offended when they are first invited to dinner overseas and told, "Don't bring the children." You need to realize that this is not a judgment against your children, but just the "way it is done". When you are invited to a social function overseas and the children are not specifically included in the invitation, be sure to ask whether they are expected before you take them. A helper can be a great help as a baby-sitter in the evenings, especially if you have a heavy schedule of evening services. Your child is much better off keeping regular bed-time hours than he would be attending church functions night after night.

One of the biggest problems of having servants who live in the home is that you must give up the privacy to which you have become accustomed. Westerners value their privacy very highly. In some cultures privacy is neither desirable nor understandable. You will have to make adjustments to having helpers living in your home. Help your servants understand that there are times and places in your home where you need privacy. You can teach them that they must always knock before entering any closed door. Or you may reserve certain places that you do not allow them to clean. For example, you may ask them not to clean your desk at all, but to leave that up to you. Or you may keep your bedroom as a separate room that you will take care of.

From the beginning have a clear employee/employer relationship with the helpers. They are not cousins coming to live with you. They are people who are hired to work in your home. It is an honorable job. Treat them with dignity and respect at all times. Some Westerners tend to treat their helpers like children. This usually is not acceptable. It does not accord proper dignity to their job.

It is important that you have a clear understanding from the beginning as to what you expect from the helper, and that the helper has a clear understanding of what is expected of him. If you hire totally untrained domestic help, remember to "show and tell" each step, many times! Sometimes a missionary expects the servant to take care of the food or the kitchen like she does, after only being told once. Remember the naked chicken! Bear in mind that you learned the particular ways that you care for the kitchen or for food over many, many years at home. Maybe your mother told you a dozen times or more before you learned to do it properly. It's too much to expect a house-helper who has done things her own way for many years to switch immediately to your way without being told over and over again. Any time that your helper does not do her job properly just kindly and clearly ask her to do it over again.

Early in our missionary life we were asked to take a young girl into our home. The family could not afford to feed her, so we were asked to take her in and teach her how to do housework. We were to provide her food and less than $5 a month. I only gave her one responsibility at first. That responsibility was to fill the water filter every night. After about a month the friend who had brought her to us (a Swiss woman who had well-trained servants) asked me, "How is Irenea doing?"

I said "Not very well. I've only given her one responsibility and she forgets it as often as she remembers it." I told her that Irenea was to fill the water filter at night before she went to bed, and she didn't always do it.

She asked me, "And what happens when she does not do it?"

I said, "Well, she's usually already asleep when I notice, so I do it."

My Swiss friend advised me, "As long as you do it, it's not necessary for her to do it regularly. The next time she forgets to do it, go to the room and call her, even if she's asleep. Tell her to come and fill the water filter."

Of course the next night she forgot. It was very hard for me to do, but I woke her and said, "I guess you forgot to fill the filter. Please fill it now." She never forgot again! That was a good lesson to me as a young missionary. If you do the work for a servant when they don't do it right, they will be happy to let you continue doing it. But if you teach them, patiently and kindly, that always, everytime they do it wrong, they must re-do it the right way, they will quickly learn.

You may need to adjust the way you think some things should be done. For example, the Asian way to wash dishes is to wash them with soap in cold water and, only if you feel it's necessary, then rinse them in hot water. The American way is to wash them in very hot water, rinse them in very hot water and then drain them. Many missionaries experience great frustration trying to get their servants to always wash the dishes in hot water. It wasn't until we moved to a place where the standard of living was so high we no longer had help that I realized that when the temperature is 35°C. and the humidity is 98 percent it is *very* hot to stand over a pan of hot dishwater! I learned to wash them in cold soapy water, then rinse them in hot water. After all, the Asian way is best in the tropics!

Clear communication with your helper is necessary to avoid problems. It may be that you are studying language and at first cannot speak the same language as your servants. You must show them everything. Show and tell! Remember to not raise your voice or shout at your helpers. Always speak in a kind firm voice. Always treat them with dignity. Always respect their position as an adult and as a worker.

In our first term we had friends in another mission who couldn't keep a helper more than a month or two. We helped them to find several different servants. Finally when our helper, Andres, told us their latest helper (who was his cousin) was leaving, I asked him to try to find out why.

Andres discovered, "Constancia is leaving because Sir does not like her!"

I asked, "What makes her think he doesn't like her? He told me the family all like Constancia very much."

Andres then related her "undeniable" proof, "Sir always talks loud, and slams the door after he talks to her. That clearly shows that he doesn't like her at all!"

I pointed out to Andres that our friend always talked loud and always slammed doors, even when he was laughing. Andres told Constancia that some foreigners always slam doors, even when they are not angry, and they very much wanted her to stay. Our friend quit slamming doors and kept their helper until furlough time. Watch your body language!

Never allow your children to boss the servants. Children should be taught to treat the servants in the home with the same graciousness that they treat other adults. Children should never be allowed to "talk smart" to helpers, in your home or anyone else's.

Before you hire a servant you should inquire around as to the proper pay scale so that you pay the average pay scale. You may feel that this is too low and want to give your helper more, but you will be disrupting the economy of the area if you do this. You may even confuse your helpers. They will wonder what "extras" you expect of them when you pay them such a high wage. You may soon find that you are unable to maintain that high wage, so try to pay what is expected on the local economy.

One thing that is sometimes a problem is thievery by the servant. You should never leave things out that would be an obvious temptation. If your helpers must live on a low pay scale it is unfair to leave money or valuable jewels around carelessly in front of them. Always keep cash and jewelry locked up where it would not be a temptation.

Know what you have in household supplies and keep a regular check, unless you don't mind if the servants take some. If that is the case you should let them know that it is all right if they take some.

I observed one Swiss family that always had their household things in even numbers, like ten towels, ten sheets, ten wash clothes, etc. After every laundry the servant was expected to count the things to make sure nothing was missing. It would be suggested, "Be sure to count so we'll know that no one has gotten over the fence and stolen something." Do not make direct accusations to your servants, but let them know that you are aware of what you have.

When you hire a servant, it is wisest to contact them through a third party who knows something about them. If this is not possible, be sure to take their identity card number, if the country requires its citizens to have identity cards. Also find out where their family can be contacted. I learned this the hard way!

When I needed help in Malaysia during a very busy time I hired someone who had posted a "position wanted by amah" ad on the bulletin board of the supermarket. Janet was extremely efficient and I thought I had a jewel. She had several written references of former employers who had "returned to England". Two weeks later she absconded with some of Joy's clothes, some "goodies" from our barrels, and the lovely jade ring and pendant which had been my last birthday gift from Les' mother before her death. My "jewel" and jewels were forever gone! The other missionaries said, "You have her ID number, don't you?" I hadn't even known there was such a thing. Live and learn!

If you should hire someone who turns out to be a petty thief and you're constantly losing things, then you must come to a parting of ways. It can be a serious problem to try to discharge a helper. You must be sure to give them the proper advance warning or severance pay. Be sure to check the labor laws of the country and also the prevailing customs regarding domestic workers, so you do not fail in any way to treat your servant properly.

When you hire someone to work in your home you do become more vulnerable to certain problems. On the other hand, a faithful servant can be a blessing to you in many ways. You will begin to understand how it could be said of Joseph (when he was a servant in Egypt) that his master "put him in charge of his houshold and of all that he owned."[4]

An honest and loyal servant may save you as much money in household management as you pay him in salary. He knows where and how to bargain for the best buys. In many places commodity prices are automatically increased when a foreigner is buying.

Servants can help you to understand nuances of cultural difference that you might otherwise miss. They help you with your langauge learning also.

With your daily Christian example in the home, your servants can see that "Christ living within" does indeed make a difference. I personally know many servants of missionaries who have become stalwart Christians. Some have become ministers of the Gospel. The children of others have become leaders in the church. Except for Janet, our helpers contributed immeasurably to our happy home life and to our ministry overseas. Flora Marfil, who helped us four years both in our home and church work; Andres and Lucing Sitjar who helped us six years in the house, yard and Bible school campus; and Kong Kai Hoong who worked for us five years, were true "Joseph" and "Josephines" to whom we could entrust everything we owned. Help your servants to be your help!

19. *Amoebas Unlimited*

Most mission boards only approve candidates who are in good health. So when you first become a missionary you will probably be in excellent condition. Let's hope that won't be the last time! Some missions require their missionaries to have an annual checkup. This is a postive aid to their missionaries. Other missions do not ask for an annual checkup, but require a complete physical during every home leave. Therefore, missionaries probably have more regular physical checkups than other American ministers!

There are a number of precautions you need to take in your daily living. One missionary doctor told us that if people would always wash their hands before they eat and before and after they use the toilet they would eliminate many of their illnesses. Such a simple precaution! Particularly if you live in the tropics where high humidity and temperatures accelerate bacteria growth, be generous with soap. The slightest scratch or skin abrasion, that you would pay little attention to in a temperate climate, can rapidly become an ugly sore if it is not washed carefully with soap and rinsed with clear water. If you are not sure your water supply is pure, use 3% hydrogen peroxide to clean a wound.

Shortly after we arrived for our second term, David fell and scraped his shin. It didn't bleed at all. The outer skin layer was just barely scraped. I washed it, disinfected it, covered it with a band-aid, and forgot it. A few days later it was very itchy. We removed the bandaid and found a raw suppurating abscess. The doctor had to dress it alternate days for about two weeks before it healed. Disinfect regularly!

You would be wise to buy a good health book that is easy to read. A book that helped me a lot when our children were small was *Better Homes and Gardens Baby Book*.[5] I still refer to it when mothers of young children ask for advice concerning a symptom or complaint with one of their children. In the section titled "Common Diseases and Complaints", the book has a chart that lists diseases, with their cause, incubation period, symptoms, duration, and recommended treatment. I referred to this quick-reference chart many times, for my own children and for other mothers. For example, it helps you to determine whether a rash is of fleeting concern or might be serious. "Is it a symptom of measles (rubeola), German measles (rubella), scarlet fever, roseola, prickly heat, or allergy?" Of course you will take a child with a rash to the doctor if one is near. But if the doctor is 180 miles away by a rough road, two hours by boat, or a six mile hike, it is helpful to be able to identify a fleeting rash yourself!

One of the "Macmillan Tropical Community Health Manuals", *Where There Is No Doctor*,[6] is useful for anyone, and especially helpful for someone located in a remote area.

It helps with many health problems that are common to the tropics, and would not be included in a book written for a temperate zone country. Subjects that will be especially helpful to missionaries are "Home Cures and Popular Beliefs", "Sicknesses That are Often Confused", "How To Take Care of a Sick Person", and "Prevention: How to Avoid Many Sicknesses" (including parasites, trichinosis, and amoebas).

The "The Home Medicine Kit" chart from this book (see following pages) is reprinted here to help you prepare in advance for your family's medical needs.

A helpful book we recently bought is *Take Care of Yourself*.[8] Its section on "The Patient and the Common Complaint" asks questions about your symptoms and, according to your "Yes" or "No" answers, advises home treatment or tells you to see a doctor. It helps you to decide quickly whether you can handle the problem yourself or actually need medical help. This is a book I advise any missionary to take with him when he goes overseas.

A section in this book titled "The Home Pharmacy" (see page 84) lists the common, scientific and brand names of effective medical supplies for treatment of common health care problems. The table reprinted here advises you on the medications you might need. These supplies will be available in most any city. If you will be living in a remote area, take these supplies with you from the nearest city. In addition, take rectal and oral thermometers, a hot water bottle, and a rubber nose syringe if you have a baby.

THE HOME MEDICINE KIT[7]

Each family should have the following things in their medicine kit. These supplies and medicines should be enough to treat many common problems in rural areas.

Also include useful home remedies in your medicine kit.

SUPPLIES

Use	Supply	Price (write in)	Amount recommended
FOR WOUNDS AND SKIN PROBLEMS:			
	sterile gauze pads in individual sealed envelopes	_____	20
	1-,2-, and 3-inch gauze bandage rools	_____	2 each
	clean cotton	_____	1 small package
	adhesive tape (adhesive plaster), 1-inch wide roll	_____	2 rolls
	disinfectant soap (like *Dial, Betadine,* or *Phisohex*	_____	1 bar of small bottle
	70% alcohol	_____	¼ liter
	hydrogen peroxide, in a dark bottle	_____	1 small bottle
	petroleum jelly *(Vaseline)* in a jar or tube	_____	1
	white vinegar	_____	½ liter
	sulfur	_____	100 gm.
	scissors (clean, not rusty)	_____	1 pair
	tweezers with pointed ends	_____	1 pair
FOR MEASURING TEMPERATURE:			
	thermometers for mouth for rectum	_____	1 each
FOR KEEPING SUPPLIES CLEAN:			
	plastic bags	_____	several

MEDICINES

Use	Medicine (generic name)	Local brand (write in)	Price (write in)	Amount recommended
FOR BACTERIAL INFECTIONS:				
	1. Penicillin, 250 mg. tablets	_____	_____	40
	2. A sulfonamide 500 mg. tablets	_____	_____	100
	3. Ampicillin, 250 mg. capsules	_____	_____	24
FOR WORMS:				
	4. Piperazine, tablets or syrup	_____	_____	40 tablets of 500 mg. or 2 bottles
FOR FEVER AND PAIN:				
	5. Aspirin, 300 mg. (5 grain) tablets	_____	_____	50
FOR DEHYDRATION:				
	6. Sodium bicarbonate (also salt and sugar)	_____	_____	½ kg.
	or prepackaged mix for rehydration drink	_____	_____	10 envelopes
FOR ANEMIA:				
	7. Iron (ferrous sulfate), 200 mg. pills (best if pills also contain vitamin C and folic acid)	_____	_____	100
FOR SCABIES AND LICE:				
	8. Lindane (gamma benzene hexa-chloride)	_____	_____	1 bottle
FOR ITCHING AND VOMITING:				
	9. Promethazine, 25 mg. tablets	_____	_____	12
FOR MILD SKIN INFECTIONS:				
	10 .Gentian violet, small bottle; or an antibiotic ointment	_____	_____	1 bottle 1 tube
FOR EYE INFECTIONS:				
	11. Antibiotic eye ointment	_____	_____	1 tube

TABLE 1

YOUR HOME PHARMACY[9]

Items in bold print are basic requirements. Other preparations may find use in some households. Keep all medicines out of the reach of children.

Ailment	Medication
Allergy	Antihistamines
	Nose drops and sprays
Colds and Coughs	Cold tablets/cough syrups
Constipation	Milk of magnesia, bulk laxatives
Dental problems (preventive)	Sodium flouride
Diarrhea	**KAOPECTATE, pagegoric**
Eye irritations	Eye drops and artifical tears
Hemorrhoids	Hemorrhoid preparations
Páin and fever	**ASPIRIN, acetaminophen**
(in children)	†**LIQUID ACETAMINOPHEN, aspirin**
	rectal suppositories
Poisoning (to induce vomiting)	†**SYRUP OF IPECAC**
Fungus	Antifungal preparations
Sunburn (preventive)	Sunscreen agents
Sprains	**ELASTIC BANDAGES**
Stomach, upset	**ANTACID, nonabsorbable**
Wounds (minor)	**ADHESIVE TAPE, BANDAGES**
(antiseptic)	**HYDROGEN PEROXIDE, IODINE**
(soaking agent)	**SODIUM BICARBONATE (baking soda)**

†Daggered items are for homes with small children.

The simple rules for good health apply overseas the same as in America. They may not be quite so easy to achieve. Be sure to get adequate rest. If you live in the tropics where everyone rests at mid-day, learn to take a siesta. This brief rest at the hottest time of the day gives you added energy later. And you won't irritate your neighbors by bothering them during the siesta hour!

Drink sufficient water. In very hot weather keep boiled water ready for babies and small children. Offer a baby 2 ounces of boiled water in a sterile bottle two or three times a day. If you will be living in the tropics take with you a gallon thermos with a spigot. Fill it with clean cold water every morning and place it where the children can easily help themselves to a drink. Have a drinking glass for each member of the family. Decorate the pre-schooler's glass with a pretty decal so he can identify it, or use different colors. You will save energy by avoiding constant opening of the refrigerator door. The children will be more likely to drink enough to replenish the water lost through perspiration if they can get their own drinks.

If you are not absolutely sure of the purity of your water supply, either boil it or use a water filter or both. If you live where amoebic dysentery is common give your children only boiled water. Make every effort to avoid recurring infection with amoeba. Small children can quickly dehydrate to a dangerous degree from prolonged diarrhea. Be careful!

I am deeply concerned for the present and future health of our missionary families who struggle with repeated bouts of amoebic dysentery. Find the source and eliminate it. Investigate your water supply. Eat only cooked vegetables. Carrots grow easily world-wide and are an excellent source of Vitamin A and iron. Unfortunately, the xylem (inner core) of raw carrots is also an excellent source of amoeba. Raw lettuce and cabbage are also culprits. If your children don't like cooked carrots, try grating them (in a blender if you have one) and cooking just 5 minutes.

Eat balanced meals. You don't have to eat the same specific foods you ate in America, but do try to get the general basic foods: cereal, fruit, vegetables, protein, milk products. In many parts of the world fresh milk is not available at all. This worries mothers. It needn't. Powdered milk is usually available. If you mix half whole and half skim milk powder and chill it overnight it tastes much like the 2% milk many families buy in America. Some people suggest that adding a drop of vanilla or a tiny bit of sugar makes it taste more like fresh milk. The easiest way to mix the milk is in a blender.

When we have lived where fresh milk is available, but very expensive, I have resorted to the subterfuge of buying one quart of milk, and stretching it . . . and stretching it . . . with powdered milk, to please the finicky taste of a guest who "can only drink fresh milk"! This little trick might help your older children make the adjustment to powdered milk. Younger children seldom notice any difference unless you point it out.

If you live where milk is not available at all, or you don't have refrigeration to keep it, some other foods supply the same food values. Cabbage (kale and collards, too), greens (mustard, turnip, beet, dandelion or spinach) and broccoli supply amounts of calcium and vitamins almost equal to that of milk. Bananas and papaya supply the same vitamins, but little calcium. You could supplement your meals with calcium tablets. Calcium is also plentiful in oysters, shrimp, and sardines.

If vitamins are not available where you will be stationed, take them with you. Our first term a friend who was selling food supplements gave us a year's supply of vitamins and minerals. When the supply dwindled Les unobtrusively quit taking them, so they would last longer for the children and me. After a few months cracks formed in the lining of his mouth. When eating became painful he saw the doctor. Vitamin deficiency! Three shots of Vitamin B complex healed the fissures. The doctor advised him to take vitamins as long as he lived in the tropics. He said Les needed them more than we did, because of his extra size and heavy schedule. The doctor told us that though we ate plenty of vegetables, because they grow so fast in the tropics they aren't as rich in vitamins or minerals as the foods to which we were accustomed

Nuts and beans are a good source of protein when meat is scarce. peanuts grow abundantly in much of Asia and Africa. If your family are peanut butter lovers you can easily make your own in a blender. Use 1 to 3 tablespoons vegetable oil in 1 cup fresh roasted or salted peanuts. If the peanuts are unsalted, add about one-half teaspoon salt per cup of nuts.

In the past it was quite common for missionaries to take large supplies of canned food with them from America. This practice is changing due to greatly increased freight costs and greater availability of "familiar" foods overseas. There may be a few special things you want to take, especially your first time. But, generally speaking, it is better to use food that is locally available.

The storage time for foods, especially in the tropics, is short. They may taste and look all right but have no food value after a few months. Most foods should be stored in a cool, dark, dry place. In the tropics a cool, dry place is difficult to find. Hence stored foods lose food value more quickly than in a temperate climate.

If you take some dry foods with you (cereals, cake mixes, jello), seal them in tin cans before you leave the temperate zone. They will last much longer in metal than in paper packages. General guidelines for maximum storage times are:

Up to 3 years: Bitter chocolate, angel food cake mix in sealed cans

Up to 2 years: whole pepper, salt, sugar

Up to 18 months: canned meats, vegetables, chicken, non-citrus fruits, dried beans, and peas

Up to 1 year: Canned fish, fats, oils, cereals, nuts, puddings, boullion products, baking soda and baking powder, spices

Up to 6 months: Canned baking powder cake mixes, dry milk, condensed soups, citrus fruits, tomatoes, sauerkraut

If the temperature averages below 25° C where you live the storage time will be extended. If it's regularly above 35° C it may be shortened.

There may be a few items you take, or buy in a city you occasionally visit, that you prize enough to keep in the freezer. I always bought whole wheat flour when I could and stored it in the freezer of our refrigerator for those special times when we wanted whole wheat rolls. I now buy Chinese walnuts in season and store them all year in the freezer.

Learn to substitute local foods for what you were accustomed to eating in America. One of my missionary friends became so adept in cooking all the local foods in a delicious way that the local women asked her to give them cooking lessons! Taste the new fruits and vegetables in small amounts at first. As you adjust to the exotic new flavors you'll be delighted with your delectable discoveries. Forever after, on furlough you'll yearn for mango, rambutan, bread fruit, or durian.

Many women are frustrated cooks when they first go overseas because they are accustomed to using prepared instant mixes. Even their cookbooks say to use certain mixes. A cookbook I discovered in the Philippines tells you how to make everything "from scratch". *Joy of Cooking,*[10] a large cookbook, is now also in paperback. It tells you "all about" foods and explains why you need to treat them certain ways. All recipes are "from scratch". You won't need mixes.

Here are a few substitutes I learned to use for traditional holiday season recipes. Jelled salads often call for celery. If celery is not available use bean sprouts. Blanch them a couple of minutes to remove the bean taste. They provide the same crisp texture that celery gives to jelled salads. Hard yellow squashes make good "pumpkin pie". Green mangoes substitute for apples in "applesauce" or "apple pie". You can combine grated, drained summer squash (zucchini or marrow) with sugar, crushed pineapple, lime juice and packaged jello to make "orange", "peach" or "apricot" marmalade. Try substituting local nuts for pecans in recipes.

Recreation is also important to your health. Establish regular times of exercise. Different people like to do different things. You should do what you most enjoy doing, because you will be more consistent in it. If you're in a hot country it may be easy for you to find a place to swim regularly. If you're in cooler country you may want to walk or run. You need not do anything expensive, but if you enjoy sports you can find some local sport to play. You can usually play tennis or some other sport that's easy to play without a team.

If your children are sports-minded, help them find a group of youngsters with whom they can play. If they are in a school system it will meet their recreation sports needs. If they study at home, it is important that you supply the sports enthusiasm and interest for them in the family. It is good to have some kind of daily sports activity for at least 15 to 30 minutes, even a walk. At least once a week, when you can take a little longer, get your mind off of your work and relax with some type of physical activity you enjoy. A hike, a swim, or a run is very good.

I personally believe that everyone should take at least a two-week vacation every year, when you get away from your work and do something entirely different. Relax, travel, have a time away from your regular responsibilities. I regret to say that we have not done this very often! But I observe that it helps people when, for at least two weeks a year, they go to a different locality away from their regular responsibilities. If you live in the city, a simpler way of life is refreshing. One lovely vacation we had as a family was in a little *nipa* house up in the hills. If you live in a remote area, you'll enjoy a trip to the city. Choose what your family enjoys, and do it on an annual basis.

If you never take a break, you may be headed for a health breakdown. Maybe not. Perhaps you thrive on your work. You may love your ministry and not want to leave it for a minute! If you are that kind of person, remember that other members of your family may not be. They may very much want a time of relaxing with you away from the responsibilities that demand your constant attention at home.

20. *Angels Unawares*

Before you went overseas, if you were a pastor in America, you probably were accustomed to a very busy social life with many visitors. You may find a drastic change when you go overseas. You may go to an area where you are quite remote. The only people you will regularly see will be those people who live right in your village.

On the other hand, if you live in a large city there may be times when you will entertain a different set of visitors each day in the week. You may have visitors in your home for months at a time. Your attitude towards this situation will determine whether you can enjoy it or whether it becomes an endurance test.

If you live in a country where you're expected to have household help it is much easier to have frequent company. You will have people to help with the cooking, the cleaning, and the laundry. But in many cities where there are many visitors, no household help is available. So the wife can become a servant who does little but cook, wash, and clean, if she devotes her full time to receiving guests. If you live in a large city and cannot get anyone to help you with the work, you probably are also in an area where hotels are easily available. It is advisable for you in this case to encourage many of the visitors who are strangers or very casual acquaintances to stay in a hotel. You do need some time to accomplish the ministry for which you have come. And you need some time with your family!

Remember though that every guest coming through may feel that you certainly have time for him! He may be a pastor or a member of one of your supporting churches who has never traveled overseas before. This is a big trip for him, a very important occasion. He may be an official in your denomination. His visit is important to him and it is also important to you. What the visitor does not know is that you had another visitor yesterday, another the day before and another each day of last week! Remember that for each visitor, it is his special trip, and try to treat the trip with the same enthusiasm. On the other hand, you must also be honest with your visitors. Let them know if you cannot spare time for sight-seeing. If you are in an area where tours are available, encourage your guests to take a commercial tour. They will learn more from it, and this will give you some time for your regular ministries.

If you live in a remote area where people do not "pass by", but come to your place only when they come to see *you,* you still may have a constant flow of visitors. When they come there may be no place to stay except with you.

Our first term we were the only missionaries of our denomination living on a large island of two provinces. During our first year there we had a steady stream of visitors for four months. Every night someone slept at our house; we never sat down to one meal without a guest. Some stayed two days, some a week, one stayed seven weeks. They were missionaries, evangelists, district leaders, U.S. military off a ship in port, friends, and strangers! We loved it. We had good household help! And we were new at it. After a few years I tried to space guests a little, so the family could have some time alone.

When Les taught a seminar class at Northwest College on "The Missionary Family", he asked our good friend, Huldah Buntain, to speak to the class about "entertaining guests". With their well-known "Mission to Calcutta", Mark and Huldah Buntain have more guests "passing through" than anyone I know.

Huldah said, "We've had the tall and the short, the fat and the thin, the young and the old . . . all have different personalities and different fields of service and ministry." They have medical students and nurses visiting the hospital. Tourists who have heard of their feeding program stop to see their ministry to children. Secretaries and young people training for the ministry have also gone to Calcutta to help them for a short term. Many pastors, evangelists and church administrators pass through Calcutta. Huldah says, "We find their ministry always encourages our people and they, too, enjoy being here to see the different phases of the work."

She says, "For many visitors it is a tremendous adjustment. There is always a water shortage, and often no fans or air conditioning due to frequent electric power cuts." At 40°C. heat you notice that! One inventive guest told them at breakfast that he had sat in the bathtub all night to keep cool. Fortunately it was filled with water (for storage).

Huldah said their apartment is like a hotel. But, in spite of Calcutta's many problems (it has been named the disaster city of 1981) their guests seem genuinely sorry to leave, because of the wonderful people that live there and the warm spirit they feel in the church. She continues, "We are grateful for all that visit Calcutta and for their love and interests shown in our work after they return to their home."

Mark and Huldah have, by necessity, learned the secret of carrying on with their work and enjoining their guests as assistants. Some people can manage this much better than others. I'm still trying to learn.

Huldah said the verse of Scripture they took as their guideline for "people passing through" is: "Do not forget to entertain strangers, for by so doing some people have entertained angels without knowing it".[11] This has proven true of many of their visitors, for they have been angels of mercy, who provide food for the hungry children, help to build churches, or give to other urgent needs.

For the last six years Les and I have had to reverse our "host-guest" roles. We rarely entertain guests because we are seldom home anymore. Since our ministry covers seven countries, we travel up to 80 percent of the time. We are usually the guests! I hope we can be "angels" to those we visit.

If your ministry makes you a guest more often than a host or hostess, here are a few guidelines for you.

Make every effort to avoid disrupting the work schedule of the people you visit. Don't ask them to take you sight-seeing or shopping. If they volunteer, fine. Don't ask.

Pay your own way. If you are coming for a long stay give your hosts money to cover your food, utilities, etc. for a week when you arrive, and weekly thereafter. Don't make them borrow money to take care of your needs, even if you intend to give them something when you leave. Don't make them worry about their grocery bill.

I know one missionary family who had to sell their air conditioner to pay the grocery bill for some evangelists who spent a month with them. Their mission clearly advises evangelists going overseas to "pay their own way", but these men said of their hosts, "They have plenty of money. They didn't ask us for any, and we ate like kings!" They never knew the family then had to manage in the constant heat without air conditioning for another year to pay for their guests' "royal meals".

Never say, "What do I owe you?" Many missions in many countries set very clear "hospitality rates". This is helpful. Nevertheless, most missionaries, as badly as they may need it, find it difficult to accept overt "payment" for room and board. Paul's command[12] to "practice hospitality" and Peter's admonition[13] to "offer hospitality to one another without grumbling", in regard to "God's people who are in need" condition us to reject payment also from people who can well afford to pay their own way. You should give a reasonable amount to cover your costs, and give it in an unobtrusive manner that can't be easily refused.

If the host's staff or household help have served you, also offer something for them. Do not give it directly to them, but to your hosts. They may have already paid the helpers extra for helping you. Their staff's services to "Christians passing through" may be included in their salary. The host may need the help to pay their salary.

Help in the ministry of the persons you visit if you can. If you can't, try to be a prayerful and out-of-the-way observer. As you pray for the family in the homes you stay in, the Lord will show you ways that you can be "angels, without (their) knowing it".

21. Separation

One of the special problems that missionaries face is the problem of separation from family members. We talked about this in unit 2. Your feelings of separation from your family in America are greatly intensified when you are ten thousand miles away. However, you should bear in mind that you are not unique. Not only missionaries, but thousands of other people leave their extended family to go to another land for various reasons. This has happened since the earliest days of history. It is not a unique problem. Yet it is something that some people cannot handle. It is something you may need to "work at". It doesn't come naturally to all people.

A very small minority of people cannot adjust to the separation from their homeland and extended family. They struggle for a year or two, or one term, then make the painful decision to go "home" and stay.

In the plant world most plants can be successfully transplanted and thrive in their new setting. A few cannot. Perhaps that is true of a few people, too. They can be productive, successful Christian workers in their home setting. Transplanted to a distant, strange location, they cease to be productive. For these few missionaries who can't cope in an alien place and feel compelled to "return home" early in their career, acceptance of their limitations will help them to take root back in their homeland and once again have a fruitful "stateside" ministry.

Missionaries remaining at their post also need to accept the limitations of the "leaving" missionaries. Give them loving support during the difficult final days of separation from the mission.

The separations that come within the nuclear family during your overseas ministry present different challenges to adjustment. One type of separation occurs because the husband's or wife's ministry requires travel. In some cases this is an occasional thing and is not a problem. It's only a short break in routine and is not something you need to worry about. But if a member of the family is required to travel away from the rest of the family for long periods of time, or frequently for short periods, this is something that will need your special attention.

Perhaps the missionary father is an evangelist. Most of his work will be away from home. If the father is an executive for his mission, within the country, or within an area, he may need to be away from home as much as half the time, or even three-fourths of the time. This is a situation with which the family must cope.

Certain procedures are advisable. The husband and wife need to keep in touch as closely as possible while the husband is traveling. You can write letters to each other, unless he is only staying in one place a day or two at a time. If you're in an area where telephones are available, you should phone on a regular basis. Then the wife knows when to expect a phone call and can be prepared with whatever information she may need to convey to the husband. The most important reason for the regular contact is the reassurance that you miss each other. You are saying, "Even though our work requires us to be apart, it is not what we wish. We would rather be together."

Perhaps it's possible for the wife to travel with the husband on occasion. But if you have toddlers or school children at home, this should be delayed for the sake of a steady home-life for the children.

Sometimes your husband must travel in remote areas where there is no way for you to stay in touch. One wife told me, "When Bud travels we *can't* contact each other. He is out in areas where there are no telephones, and he's in a different place every day. So we have a pact. Every night at 8 o'clock we pray for each other. This 'homing' through the times we are separated draws us closer to each other! We both know there is always this one time every day when we are (thinking of each other) 'together'."

When Les first started traveling, our family postponed all our special "treats" until Daddy came home. Then a woman whose husband traveled in business all the time gave me some sound advice.

She said, "Don't save all of your best foods to have when Daddy comes home. Daddy's eating company meals all the time he's gone, and your children are being deprived of those special things while Daddy's gone. Carry on your way of life as normally as possible when the husband and father has to be away. If you normally get especially dressed up and go to the beauty shop when your husband's home, do so when he's gone as well. Do fun things with the children. Swim. Go to the zoo. Let them have a slumber party. Keep alive!"

I read in an article by Ruth Graham (Mrs. Billy Graham) advice to not make a "big thing" of every farewell and return, when your husband regularly travels. Accept it and treat it as normal for him to leave and return, just as a commuting father would leave every morning and return every night.

If you make a big thing about everyone going to the airport for a tearful farewell, moping and crying because Daddy's gone, you emphasize for the children that they have a sad and unhappy life. Daddy should tell the children good-bye as if he were going off to work. Treat it as a normal way of life.

One wife whose husband has been an administrator most of their marriage told me how she used to stand at the window and cry every time he drove off. Then she would mope around the house all the time he was gone.

She told me, "Now I'm so aggravated at myself to think of all the interesting things I could have been accomplishing during that time. I wasted all those days moaning and feeling sorry for myself." And of course, by the way, putting very negative attitudes in her children's minds toward their father's ministry.

If your husband's ministry requires him to travel away from the family a lot, first of all husband and wife must mutually agree that this is the right thing for them. If they cannot come to this agreement, they should get counsel. They may even need to reconsider whether that ministry is right for them at the present time.

If the husband and wife are in agreement that this is the right ministry for him, then accept the separation as God's plan for you, and your normal way of life. Do not feel sorry for yourself. Carry on your life. Have a useful plan for what you will do while your husband travels. Make life happy and exciting for the children whether father is there or not. Then maximize "family time" when daddy is home as well.

Maintain the same pattern of discipline in the home, whether father is there or away. Avoid two traps: postponing all discipline when father is away ("You'll get it when Daddy gets home!"); or postponing all discipline when he's home ("I'm here such a short time, I don't want a confrontation with the kids!"). The first trap makes an "ogre" of the father; the second makes mother the "whip". If children need correction they need it at the time of the offense, not later. Punishment postponed either puts too heavy an anticipatory burden on the child, if always carried out; or allows misbehavior to be overlooked, if it's often forgotten. Neither is good discipline.

Many fathers, when they travel, say to their oldest son (regardless of his age). "You're the man of the house now! Take care of your mother and sister." I know this is well meant, but there is danger of its putting too heavy a burden on a small child or even a young teen. If all goes fine during Dad's absence, well and good. But what if a fire, earthquake, or riot rips your serenity? Impotent in the face of disaster, the son can be overwhelmed with a sense of failure. I think it is better if the father counsels both son and daughter to be helpful and obedient. If he builds up the mother as the authority in his absence, and praises her management on his return, the children will respect her leadership in the home.

When father travels a lot the managing of family finances needs to be worked out. One traveling missionary told me it helps to have two checking accounts. Both are joint accounts, but he uses one and she the other to avoid overdrawing when they are separated several weeks. If you can handle credit cards (paying the full amount each month to avoid interest payments) this is a great convenience to the traveler.

Decide whether husband or wife will be responsible for regular payments (rent, utilities, insurance, credit cards, children's schooling, etc., etc., etc.,). It usually works better if the wife handles the bills, since she will be at home. If the husband does it, he should anticipate all payments before he goes away and leave the prepared payments with her, ready for mailing.

Perhaps the husband can handle quarterly, semi-annual, or annual payments, with the wife managing the more frequent bills. Work out what is best for you, to avoid recriminations.

When the husband (or wife) first starts traveling there will be a major adjustment in decision-making. If the husband has been the total authority in the home, the wife can be "thrown" by suddenly having to make decisions she has always deferred to him. In some families, the wife herself had shrunk from making decisions; in others, the husband would not allow her to make any. In both cases this situation has to change when the husband starts traveling. I have never met a missionary wife who could not rise to the need in this situation.

Perhaps the greatest adjustment in this area is in working out the family decision-making roles during the brief times when the husband is home, if the wife has to make all the decisions while he travels. The wife may be all-too-happy to drop this responsibility as soon as the husband walks in the door. However, if the husband is away more than half the time, switching roles constantly is not easy to do. Work out what is best for you, but do talk it over and consider everyone's viewpoint: husband, wife, children, and staff.

If you all agree that the husband should continue to make all important decisions, be prepared for many decisions to be postponed again and again, and much to be left undone during his absences.

When Les' ministry began to keep him away from home for three weeks or longer at a time, we observed that a "reunion pattern" emerged. Best of all was the honeymoon phase: everyone happy and loving, thrilled to be together again. About the third day after the family was reunited, our idyll would be disrupted. A difference of opinion over a minor decision, or conflicting plans, individually made, "disturbed the peace". We soon realized that it takes a conscious effort on the part of both husband and wife to move smoothly back into "partnership planning" when each has been required, by the absence of the other, to make independent decisions over an extended time.

Perhaps the children, too, have made plans with the mother's approval, worked out "curfew hours", or even made major decisions, that are settled in all their minds. If the absence is long and letter writing is not possible, the mother can make notes of such plans or decisions to share with the father early on his return. The father, too, must be patient. He can realize that when his wife and older children are forced by his absences to make independent decisions, his respect of those decisions makes it easier for them to cope with his repeated absence. The same principles apply for coping with separations for deputation travel in your homeland.

No one likes these separations, but if you talk over the problems they create and communicate your needs to each other, you can learn to cope with them.

Because they know Les travels so much, several Asian church executives or their wives (who are newly confronted with separation) have asked me, "How do you feel about being separated so much?"

I answer, "It's the thing in our lives I like the least and dislike the most! But I can cope with it. There are aspects to any ministry or any job that are unpleasant. We deal with the unpleasant part the best we can, but we don't dwell on it, or we destroy ourselves with self-pity".

I further assure them, "I'd rather have Les 50 percent of the time than anyone else in the world all the time!"

Another separation that Americans overseas dread is their children's leaving home for school in America. Europeans accept their children's departure much more readily, because children have "gone away" to boarding school for centuries in Europe. They often are quite amused at Americans who get tearful about their children leaving when they're 18 years old!

When your children are small you may think you will never be able to bear the separation, but as your children mature and reach college age you will find that they are ready to go and it is easier to let them go than you had anticipated.

Our daughter was the first in our family to leave. It was during the time of the Vietnam war, and I was very much aware that if she were a son, and 18 years old, she would probably be going to war. I was so thankful she was only going away to college it helped me to accept the separation more easily.

Your children will probably be eager to go. If they are mature and have been encouraged to make their own decisions and take care of themselves, it may be very easy for them to leave. It is harder for the mother and father to turn loose. Try to think back to when you were 18 and wanting to get out on your own. It will help you to understand that your children are ready to go. When they are gone, keep in touch with them by correspondence and by telephone calls, especially on their birthdays and special holidays. But don't cling too tightly!

Parents who have the greatest difficulty adjusting to their "empty nest" seem to be from two kinds of families. One is where the children have been neglected to "put the work first". Suddenly the parents realize it is too late to spend time with their children. These parents often grieve inordinately the "loss" of a child to college. Hold precious the hours with your small children, then let them go when they are older and ready to "fly away". Your attention to them earlier gives both of you the confidence for the separation later.

Parents who have neglected each other, to always "put the children first" can have onerous difficulty adjusting to the empty nest. They may find thay have nothing to say to each other! Guard all your relationships within the family in the children's growing up years. Remember that you had only each other before the children came, and will likely have only each other again, after they leave. One delighted wife told me, "I found out that 'mother and father' left when our three children did, but 'sweethearts' were still here!" If you have neglected your husband/wife relationship, begin now to restore it. In so doing you will build your own and the children's confidence for the empty nest separation.

The dreaded final separation that we need to discuss is the death of a family member. We never anticipate the death of our children. Thankfully, few missionary children die in these days, with greatly improved health care overseas. But it does happen. When a child dies, your grief is intensified by your isolation. There is no extended family to offer their support. If you are the only missionary in a remote region, each family member occupies a very large space in your social life. What a dreadful loss to lose a child! I have never experienced this, but I have lost three much desired, long-term pregnancies. The grace of God can sustain us through the difficult days of overwhelming loss. He can undergird and strengthen us.

A tragedy we all hope to avoid, but should nevertheless prepare for is the death of a spouse. Doctors Thomas Holmes and Richard Rahe, psychiatrists at the University of Washington Medical School in Seattle, devised a scale of events in life that cause stress. According to their scale, the most stressful event that can happen to anyone is the death of a spouse. If you live thousands of miles from all the rest of your family, it adds to the stress. You feel totally alone.

If the wife dies, the husband may have the attention-occupying comfort of his work. If he lives in an area where there is household help, or he lives in a large community of missionaries, he will have people to help him. But he has lost the one person with whom he has shared himself fully, perhaps for many years. It is extremely difficult to go through this separation.

When a wife loses her husband, if she also has a call and a personal desire to be a missionary, she may be able to continue her work. On the other hand, it may be that the work they were doing was based totally on her husband's gift of ministry. She may not be able to continue in the work or in her home. She faces a complete relocation: home, country, job, friends, church.

Five years ago, I met a lovely missionary who had recently lost her husband. When she read Holmes and Rahe's list of stress-causing changes she exclaimed, "No wonder it has been such a difficult year! By this list I see that I have just gone through twelve of the more stressful environmental changes. I've lost my husband. I have lost my work. My marriage status has changed: I'm now a widow. I had to move, not only to a new job, but also to a new country. I had to learn a whole new kind of ministry. My financial state has been greatly reduced. My total responsibilities are changed. My living conditions are drastically changed. I've had to revise my personal life habits. I've had to change my work hours and conditions. I had to go through all these changes because of the loss of my husband."

There is no way you can prepare for the heartache and pain the loss of a spouse brings. But while you still have each other there are things you can do to make it a little easier to deal with the immediate and future problems that follow death.

Discuss together and each of you decide and put in writing whether you would want to be buried overseas if you die there. Send a copy of this decision to the immediate members of your stateside family. If you have not informed them of your decision, they could resent your spouse's failure to ship your body "home" for burial.

Both husband and wife should make a will. If there are minor children, name their guardian in the event you should both die. Discuss this first with the guardians you choose, to be sure they are willing to take the responsibility. Your children are your most precious possession. Plan for their care.

Carry enough insurance to cover death expenses and the care of minor children, unless you have adequate resources for these needs. Social security is one resource for the care and education of minor children.

State in your will what should be done with your personal belongings in case of your death.

In writing (not in your will, since this would be subject to frequent change) state who you would like to dispose of your belongings. Give this statement to your immediate superiors in your mission or church.

Death is something we need to prepare for, but we hope will never come to us or our loved ones. When it does come, we find our consolation in the sure knowledge that we will meet again, with Christ, in heaven. We face the changes that must come, and know that God will strengthen us for the necessary adjustments. We can know also that our family-in-Christ are aware of our needs, wishing to help us, and praying for us.

A missionary friend who was widowed shared with me the overwhelming loneliness she experienced. For her I wrote the following poem which she asked me to share with others.

THE WIDOW
Copyright 1979 by Jo Kenney

Thirty years we grew
    Side by side.
Straight young trees,
Reaching up and out
    Together.

Our branches embraced
    Each other.
Two maturing trees,
Interlaced, supporting,
    Secure.

The Gardener came
    Unannounced.
One tree . . . uprooted, torn . . .

Stripping, peeling, leaving me
    Shorn.

Winter shivered my
    Barren limbs.
One wounded tree,
Desolate and cold,
    Alone.

The Gardener nurtured
    Struggling roots.
One trembling tree,
Warming, bearing tiny shoots,
    Alive!

22. Farewell

A young missionary wittily observed, "Old missionaries in the Far East don't retire; they are disOriented!"

Indeed, some missionaries don't retire. Some do become "disoriented"; but some continue effective ministry overseas until their death. I know one 81-year-old missionary who is still very active, and well-loved by the people she serves. Perhaps that is the clue: she *serves*. Those missionaries who cannot retire because they *rule,* and cannot relinquish their power, disserve their constituents.

I read in a business magazine that a company in which the older leadership "hangs tightly to the reins," refusing to make room for younger leaders, will lose its foreward momentum. A missionary who is afraid to retire "for the work's sake" needs to judge his feelings carefully. Is he afraid to "entrust to reliable men who will also be qualified to teach others"?[14] Or is he truly needed to carry on a ministry no one else can perform?

If the national church you serve and your missionary fellowship both urge you to remain beyond retirement age, you have a choice. But if you have to "fight" for your "right" to stay, carefully consider whether it might be time to "hand the reins" to another (either a national leader or a younger missionary.)

Some missionaries would like to retire, but are laden with guilt when they consider it. They have worked hard and ministered faithfully for 35, 40, or more years. They don't know how to slow down. Maybe they worry that the church (overseas or "back home") will think they have "let them down" if they retire. They need to be reassured by their co-workers, the "host church" and the "sending church", that their "right" to retire is fully understood and respected. The sending church could have a special "appreciation time" at their annual conference for missionaries who have served a determined number of years, when they let those missionaries know that the church considers that they have "finished the race" and "kept the faith".[15]

If you belong to a large, long-established mission, retirement plans are usually well prepared for you. Some missions suggest retirement at age 65 or after 30 years of service. Others consider age only.

If your mission does not have an adequate retirement program, you need to plan ahead for retirement. Set aside a regular amount of your salary every month toward those "leaner" years. If you are self-employed, look into the individual retirement plans that are recognized by the government.

By the time you are in your 50's it is good to start thinking about where you will be located on retirement. One missionary approaching retirement told me their greatest concern was to find a place to live that they could afford. Rather poignantly she mused, "If we had a home to go to, we wouldn't have to go so soon." They would have liked to stay another year, but to hope to qualify for their provincial government housing for retirees, they had to be in their home area, living with relatives, for a certain length of time before they could apply for the house. She said, "If only we'd bought a small house years ago and rented it out while we were overseas, we could stay longer now. As it is, we can't wait, but must go now." That was after 46 years as missionaries!

Some churches in America provide an apartment for retiring missionaries. If a church is planning to do this, it will be very helpful to the missionary if they can tell them *before* they come home at retirement age.

Another retiring missionary advised younger missionaries: keep up your insurance and keep your home when you go overseas if you can manage it. Most of the retired missionaries I interviewed said, "We were so sure the Lord would return before we got old that we saw no necessity of planning for retirement." New missionaries today feel this same imminence of the Lord's return. We need to witness for Christ with the urgency of His return "tomorrow", but prepare for the future in the event He delays "yet a little while."

I am deeply grateful to the retiring and retired missionaries who gave the following helpful hints to pass on to you:

1. *Prepare for "re-entry shock":*
   —Be aware that leaving will hurt. Expect the "final departure blues". Ask the Lord to help at this crucial transition time.
   —Ask trusted friends to pray with you.
   —Remember that *you* are different and must adjust.
   —Learn the language! To be "at home" you need to learn new words and phrases (and "unlearn" some old ones.) You also need to relate to small talk topics: gardening, inflation, energy shortage, the neighbor's dogs, etc. Be aware that few people want to hear about Asia or Africa in casual conversation.
   —Allow yourself time for "laying your memories to rest". Know that your adjustment may take up to a year. Be patient.

2. *Put your overseas experience to useful service:*
   —Write articles or stories about missionary life.
   —Help to plan and promote church missions conventions.
   —Serve as church correspondent to missionaries.
   —Offer to "fill in" as needed for church missions conventions in your area.
   —Keep a list of missions prayer needs, and pray until the answer comes.

—Offer to help traveling missionaries, by allowing them to use your address for a mail "drop".

—Minister to overseas students in your home.

—Entertain visiting missionaries.

—Duplicate and mail the newsletters of a missionary friend.

3. *Find active "stateside" ministry:*
—Conduct home Bible studies for your neighborhood.

—If asked, serve as deacon or other church officer.

—Be active in men's or women's mission support groups.

—Serve as church musician.

—Visit people in hospitals, prisons or retirement homes near you.

—"Keep young" by inviting young couples in the church to your home for dinner.

4. *Develop hobbies that interest you:*
—Take care of all those stamps you've collected.

—Do handwork (crochet, knit, macrame, embroidery).

—Garden (both flowers for beauty and vegetables for food).

—Read all the books you never had time to read before.

—Reread much-loved inspirational literature

—Enjoy music, as a participant or listener.

One missionary couple told me their children gave them, as a retirement gift, a console record player, tape deck, and radio, and a colored television. Nothing could have given them more hours of listening pleasure. They get five Christian radio stations, have a library of long-playing records, and are uplifted by the daily Christian TV programs. After living in countries where you cannot get Christian programs on radio or television (as we have) it is a spiritual feast to hear good Christian music or messages in your home at will.

Someone said, "If you want to know what you'll be like when you're 70 or 80, look at what you are at 30 or 40". If you have a rich fulfilling life with many interests in your younger years, you'll probably carry that flexibility into a satisfying life in retirement. If the Lord blesses you with long life, continue to share Him and His blessings with those around you, whether overseas or "back home." "Rejoice in the Lord always. I will say it again: Rejoice! Let your gentleness be evident to all. The Lord is near. Do not be anxious about anything, but in everything, by prayer and petition, with thanksgiving, present your requests to God. And the peace of God, which transcends all understanding, will guard your hearts and minds in Christ Jesus."[16]

More Learning Experiences

1. Read one of the books on money management from the Reading List. Prepare a budget for your current living expenses and follow it as training for living within the budget when you become a missionary.

2. Ask a visiting missionary who had servants overseas to discuss his experiences of living with servants, both the advantages and disadvantages.

3. Write to a missionary your group supports. Ask them if you can send them some dry food mixes to help them feed their guests, what foods they want, how they should be sent, and how frequently. Be sure to follow their directions carefully to avoid loss or high custom fee.

4. Retired missionaries are sometimes forgotten. Ask your state missions director for the names and addresses of retired missionaries near you. Send an offering to one. If you can tactfully learn their needs, surprise them with a gift shower at Christmas or on their birthday.

5. Invite one or more retired missionaries to a question-and-answer session with your group. Ask about their experiences related to the subjects in this unit. Arrange their transporation to your group meeting if necessary. Give them a love offering and pray for them at the end of the session.

6. Prepare home medical kits of the non-liquid items listed in the charts in chapter 19 to give to visiting missionaries, or to send overseas to a missionary.

Notes

PART ONE

[1] Isaiah 6:8

[2] Judges 6:11-16

[3] 2 Corinthians 12:9-10

[4] 1 Corinthians 13:4-7

[5] 1 Corinthians 7:32-34

[6] Proverbs 18:22

[7] 1 Corinthians 13:4-7

PART TWO

[1] Scovel, Myra, *To Lay a Hearth,* New York: Harper and Row, 1968, p. 59.

[2] Moore, Shirley, "You Can Have a Home Despite Frequent Moves," *Today's Health,* Volume XXXIII, pp. 40, 41, October, 1955.

[3] McGinnis, Marilyn, *Single,* Old Tappan: Spire Books, Revell, 1977, p. 140

[4] Sands, Audrey Lee, *Single and Satisfied,* see *Bibliography.*

PART THREE

[1]Deuteronomy 6:5-7

[2]Luke 6:31

[3]Exodus 21:24 (King James Version)

[4]Proverbs 22:6

PART FOUR

[1]Philippians 4:12

[2]Shedd, Charlie, *Letters to Karen,* New York: Avon Books, 1965, p. 119.

[3]"Home, Cash Safest Hedge." *Pacific Stars and Stripes,* May 22, 1980.

[4]Genesis 39:4, 5

[5]*Better Homes and Garden Baby Book* New York: Bantam Books, 1969.

[6]Werner, David, *Where There is No Doctor,* London: Macmillian, 1979.

[7]Used by permission of the Hesperian Foundation, from *Where There is No Doctor,* pp. 334, 335, by David Werner, copyright 1979 *by the Hesperian Foundation.*

[8]*Vickery, Donald M., M.D., and Fries, James F., M.D., Take Care of Yourself,* Reading, Massachusetts: Addison-Wesley, 1977.

[9]Reprinted by permission of Addison-Wesley Publishing Co., from *Take Care of Yourself,* by Donald M. Vicker, M.D., copyright 1976.

[10]Rombauer, Irma and Becker, Marion Rombauer, *Joy of Cooking,* Indianapolis: Bobbs-Merrill, 1962.

[11]Hebrews 13:2

[12]Romans 12:13

[13]1 Peter 4:9

[14]2 Timothy 2:2

[15]2 Timothy 4:7

[16]Philippians 4:4-7

Reading List - Bibliography

Bowman, George M., *How to Succeed With Your Money,* Chicago: Moody, 1974.

Collins, Marjorie A., *Manual for Accepted Missionary Candidates,* Pasadena: William Carey Library, 1972.

Condon, John C., and Yousef, Fathi S., *An Introduction to Intercultural Communication,* Indianapolis: Bobbs-Merrill, 1975.

Craig, Jo Ann, *Culture Shock* (In Malaysia and Singapore), Singapore: Times Books International, 1979.

Ebrahim, G.J., *Child Care in the Tropics,* London: Macmillan, 1979.

Edelstein, Shirlee, Editor, *Living In Hong Kong,* Hong Kong: Amcham Publications, 1979.

Gallagher, Neil, *Don't Go Overseas Until You've Read This Book,* Minneapolis: Bethany Fellowship, 1977.

Griffiths, Michael C., *Give Up Your Small Ambitions,* Chicago: Moody Press, 1971.

Hall, Edward T., *The Silent Language,* New York: Doubleday, 1959.

Herman, Dr. Carol, "MK's and Their Parents," *Emissary,* Vol. 10, No. 3, P.O. Box 794, Wheaton, Illinois, October, 1979.

Isais, Juan, *The Other Side of the Coin,* Grand Rapids: Eerdmans, 1966.

Klausner, William and Kampan, *Conflict or Communication* (In Thailand), Bangkok: Business Information and Research Company, 1979.

LeBar, Lois, *Family Devotions With School-age Children,* Old Tappan: Power Books, Revell, 1973.

Lockerbie, D. Bruce, *Education of Missionaries' Children,* Pasadena, William Carey Library, 1975.

Lockerbie, Jeannie, *By Ones and By Twos,* Pasadena: William Carey Library, 1983.

McGinnis, Marilyn, *Single,* Old Tappan: Spire Books, Revell, 1977.

MacGregor, Malcolm, *Your Money Matters,* Minneapolis: Bethany Fellowship, 1977.

Mostert, John, *The Preparation of a Missionary,* Wheaton: Accrediting Association of Bible Colleges, 1976.

Mumford, Amy Ross, *It Only Hurts Between Paydays,* Denver: Accent Books, 1980.

Nida, Eugene, *Customs and Cultures,* Pasadena, William Carey Library, 1975.

Nutritive Values of Foods, Home and Garden Bulletin, United States Department of Agriculture, Washington, D.C., 1976.

Roundhill, Kenneth S., *Prescription for Today's Missionary,* London: Marshall, Morgan and Scott, 1972.

Sands, Audrey Lee, *Single and Satisfied,* Wheaton: Tyndale, 1971.

Sargent, Douglas N., *The Making of a Missionary,* London: Hodder and Stoughton, 1960.

Scovel, Myra, *To Lay a Hearth,* New York: Harper and Row, 1968.

Strauss, Richard, *Confident Children,* Wheaton: Tyndale, 1975.

Sumichrast, Michael and Shafer, Ronald G., *The Complete Book of Home Buying*, Princeton: Don Jones Books, 1980.

Vickery, Donald M., M.D., and Fries, James F., M.D., *Take Care of Yourself*, Reading, Massachusetts: Addison-Wesley, 1977.

Werkman, Sidney, M.D., *Bringing Up Children Overseas*, New York: Basic Books, 1977.

Werner, David, *Where There Is No Doctor*, London: Macmillan, 1979. (Also available in Spanish, *Donde No Hay Doctor*, and Portuguese. Associated publishers in Delhi, Dublin, Hong Kong, Johannesburg, Lagos, Melbourne) Copyright by The Hesperian Foundation, Box 1692, Palo Alto, California, 94302. Also available through: Editorial Pax-Mexico, Rep. Argentina 9, Mexico 1, D.F. (Spanish) and Edicoes Paulinas, Caixa Postal 8107, 01000 Sao Paulo, S.P. Brazil (Portuguese).

World Fellowship Committee, *The Philippines Experience*, YWCA of the Phillipines, Manila: YWCA, 1975.